GENERAL JAMES OGLETHORPE

ENDORSEMENT

John Phillips' *General James Oglethorpe: From Georgia to Cranham Hall* has three major things to recommend it. As biographies go, it is short, informative and to the point. Oglethorpe, living from 1696 till 1785, witnessed, and was central to, some of the most important events of the eighteenth century in US-UK relations. For those who know little of his life, this book will be an eye-opener to those early days of Imperial expansion. Phillips tells a stirring tale of how one man sought justice, first in his own country and then in South Carolina and Georgia for the disadvantaged and dispossessed: underpaid Royal Navy seamen, those in debtors' prisons, those denied freedom of conscience. But more than this, Oglethorpe fought a lonely battle in attempting to found a colony that was not dependent on slavery - when every other one was.

Equally brave, both in moral and physical terms, was his insistence on fair trade with the Indians of his day and his respect for them. Few of his status would be prepared, as he was, to act as pallbearer at the funeral of an Indian chief, his close friend. To crown all this Oglethorpe was a capable military leader building chains of forts and conducting successful campaigns against the Spanish and French in keeping his community safe.

Phillips captures all this and more (his marriage and political life) in this fast-moving account of a heroic figure who loved both Britain and America, welcomed the peace after Independence and stood unflinchingly for what is right.

MARCUS PAUL
Author of *Ireland to the Wild West: A True Story
of Romance, Faith, Tragedy, and Hope*

JOHN PHILLIPS

GENERAL JAMES OGLETHORPE

From Georgia to Cranham Hall

AMBASSADOR INTERNATIONAL
GREENVILLE, SOUTH CAROLINA & BELFAST, NORTHERN IRELAND

www.ambassador-international.com

GENERAL JAMES OGLETHORPE

From Georgia to Cranham Hall
©2023 by John Phillips
All rights reserved

Paperback ISBN: 978-1-64960-339-5
eISBN: 978-1-64960-357-9

Cover Design by Hannah Linder Designs
Interior Design by Dentelle Design
Edited by Martin Wiles

Although every precaution has been taken in the preparation of this book, the publisher and author assume no responsibility for errors or omissions. Neither is any liability assumed for damages resulting from the use of information contained herein.

AMBASSADOR INTERNATIONAL
Emerald House Group, Inc.
411 University Ridge, Suite B14
Greenville, SC 29601
United States
www.ambassador-international.com

AMBASSADOR BOOKS
The Mount
2 Woodstock Link
Belfast, BT6 8DD
Northern Ireland, United Kingdom
www.ambassadormedia.co.uk

The colophon is a trademark of Ambassador, a Christian publishing company.

One, driven by strong benevolence of soul, shall fly,

like Oglethorpe from pole to pole.

—Alexander Pope[1]

TABLE OF CONTENTS

LIST OF ILLUSTRATIONS

ACKNOWLEDGMENTS

I wish to thank all who have helped me produce this book: Mr. Christopher Phillips for his comments on the draft manuscript, Mrs. Brenda Reeve for proofreading, Mr. Mike Burke for assistance with formatting, Martin Wiles from Ambassador International for editing the book and my wife, Janice, for her ongoing encouragement and support.

I gained a limited understanding of the achievements of James Oglethorpe from my headmaster at Oglethorpe County Primary School in Cranham, Essex. I learned more about his activities in early 2020 from reading, "Georgia, the Last Colony" in *Pilgrims and Adventurers*, published by the Essex Record Office in 1992 and written by an old school friend, John Smith. Mrs. Vicky Blackburn kindly provided me with detailed information about the founding of Georgia in the research conducted by the late Mr. Maynard Furze of Cranham Hall Farm, Cranham.

My further research included several books about Oglethorpe, which I ordered from the USA, along with several helpful online articles. A list of my main sources is included, and most of the content in this book can be found in at least two or more of them. I have found that the actual information can vary across the sources, and I have gone to great lengths to establish what, if, and when certain events took place. I have carefully endeavored not to use text directly from any one source and have written as much as possible in my own words. I have personally researched the sources of the quotations used in the book, which are listed in the references section.

I have obtained permission to use most of the images shown in the book. Since it has proved difficult to identify all possible remaining owners of copyright, if anyone believes they own the copyright of any of the images used in this book, I would be delighted to hear from them so I can acknowledge this in any future printings.

INTRODUCTION

In the Introduction to my previous book, *Victorian Cranham and the Boyd School*, I described how my family moved to the village of Cranham in Essex in 1950. My sister and I attended the recently opened Oglethorpe County Primary School, which has since been renamed the James Oglethorpe School. We were taught about General James Oglethorpe, the great philanthropist and founder of Georgia in the eighteenth century. The general had lived for the later part of his life at Cranham Hall, and we learned about his national prominence in promoting prison reform and founding the State of Georgia in North America for poor people who were in debt.

When the first national lockdown restrictions began in the United Kingdom in March 2020, due to the Covid-19 pandemic, I decided to find out more about James Oglethorpe. The more I read, the more I understood that he had been an extraordinary man. In 1744, his friend, Dr. Samuel Johnson, unsuccessfully urged Oglethorpe to write his biography, declaring, "I know no man whose life would be more interesting."[2] I set out to write an illustrated chronological account of his life.

This book is intended to be of educational and academic value in both the UK and USA. I include my reflections on James Oglethorpe's legacy in Georgia, followed by questions for reflection by the reader on the general's life. I hope it will also be of interest to those who enjoy reading about famous personalities of past centuries whose lives made a great impact on many people of their time.

The book has been written at a time when historians are evaluating from different perspectives the impact of the British Empire on their former colonies. James Oglethorpe entered public life at a time when the empire had expanded significantly in North America. However, he cannot be compared to later prominent empire-builders, such as Robert Clive in India and Cecil Rhodes in Africa. Oglethorpe's motivation for founding Georgia was undoubtedly philanthropic. The Georgia plan was a remarkable vision when considering the rigid class structure in Georgian society at that time.

James Oglethorpe's legacy in Georgia has been widely debated since his death, and I have tried to take a balanced view in covering both his successes and failures. Themes within the book include well-intended philanthropy—which was not necessarily effective—the abhorrent attitude toward and increasing dependence of the British Empire on slavery, and the origin of the Methodist movement in the Church of England—as seen in the time spent in Georgia by John and Charles Wesley and George Whitefield.

JAMES OGLETHORPE'S FAMILY BACKGROUND

When considering James Oglethorpe's achievements, it is important to note that he came from an aristocratic Stuart family and had a privileged military background.

The Oglethorpes had owned lands in Bramham, Yorkshire, since before the Norman Conquest, when an Oglethorpe was said to have been reeve, or high sheriff, of the county. The lands stayed in the family until James' grandfather, Sutton Oglethorpe, a prominent Royalist commander, lost them in 1653 during the English civil wars. Following the restoration of the Stuart monarchy in 1660, James' father, Sir Theophilus Oglethorpe, rose to the rank of brigadier general in the British army. However, in 1688, the Catholic king, James II, fled to France and was replaced by the Protestant William of Orange. James' father and Catholic mother, Lady Eleanor Oglethorpe, remained loyal supporters of the Royal House of Stuart, which led to the end of his father's military career.

In the late autumn of 1696, Sir Theophilus took the oath of loyalty to the new king, William III. In 1698, he was elected as a member of Parliament for Haslemere in Surrey. He died in 1702 and was succeeded in that post by his two eldest sons—first, Lewis and then, Theophilus.

Jacobites aimed to restore the exiled James II—the rightful king of England in their perception. Rumors held that Eleanor and her daughter,

Anne, held secret meetings at their Surrey residence at Westbrook Place for Jacobites, who had entered the house using a tunnel from the nearby town of Godalming. The Jacobites were seen as a serious threat to the status quo by the British Parliament throughout the first half of the eighteenth century.

James Oglethorpe appears to have also initially been influenced by his mother to support the Stuart cause but would later distance himself from it once he became prominent in public life.

PART ONE
A FAMOUS PHILANTHROPIST

EARLY LIFE

James Edward Oglethorpe was born in London on December 22, 1696. He was baptized the following day by the Archbishop of Canterbury at St. Martin-in-the-Fields Church. James was the tenth and last child of Sir Theophilus and Lady Eleanor Oglethorpe. From 1688, the Oglethorpe family lived in both Surrey and a London residence.

In 1688, the Oglethorpes purchased the Manor of Westbrook, including the original house known as Westbrook Place, near Godalming in Surrey. The original house appears to have been built soon after the restoration and since then has been considerably altered and the grounds diminished. It is now Grade II listed and has been known as The Meath Care Home since 1892.

Children during the eighteenth century had short childhoods. At ten years of age, James Oglethorpe was enrolled in Queen Anne's First Regiment of Foot Guards, a mainly ceremonial regiment. He was educated for a short while

Westbrook Place

at Eton, then, in 1714, entered Corpus Christi College at Oxford University. He did not complete his course but two years later resigned from his commission in the British army and decided to further his military career on the continent. This decision may have been influenced by the death of Queen Anne in 1714, the last Stuart monarch. She was succeeded by the Hanoverian king, George I, whose accession to the throne was followed by an unsuccessful Jacobite rebellion in 1715. Oglethorpe's sympathies at that time may have been with the Stuart cause. He went to France and entered the Lompres Military Academy near Paris, where he trained for leadership in battle.

By the seventeenth century, the Turkish Ottoman Empire had become one of the largest and most powerful empires in human history and controlled most of Southeast Europe. In 1716, it declared war on Austria, and hostilities continued for two years. Prince Eugene of Savoy, one of Europe's most famous commanders at that time, led the Austrian army.

At the age of nineteen, Oglethorpe volunteered with other young men from across Europe to join Prince Eugene's army, where he soon advanced from being a secretary to becoming the prince's aide-de-camp. In 1716, he was present at the Battle of Petrovardin and the siege of Timisoara. Prince Eugene was victorious at both. On August 3, 1717, Oglethorpe fought at the successful siege of Belgrade in Serbia, which was under Turkish control, where he was commended for his bravery. Following his successful campaign against the Turks, Oglethorpe remained in Europe the following year and visited family members

At the end of 1718, Oglethorpe returned to England and re-entered Corpus Christi College. He could read and speak Latin and loved classical literature. However, he did not graduate. In 1731, the college awarded him a special Master of Arts degree in recognition of his work on prison reform. However, his fortunes took a dramatic downturn in 1722 when he unintentionally killed a man in a brawl in London. It was decided that he had acted in self-defense, and he was sentenced to five months in prison.

Oglethorpe at Belgrade
in 1718

PARLIAMENTARY CAREER

Despite the humbling experience Oglethorpe had suffered earlier that year, in 1722, he successfully stood for the seat for Haslemere in the House of Commons. The seat had previously been held by his father and two older brothers. He was then twenty-five years of age and continued to hold the seat for thirty-two years. The attachment of James Oglethorpe's family members to the Jacobite cause was widely known, so his actions in Parliament were closely scrutinized from the beginning.

Oglethorpe made his first recorded speech on April 8, 1723. The Bishop of Rochester, Dr. Francis Atterbury, had been accused of involvement in a plot to restore James II to the English throne. This led to a bill proposing he be banned from living in this country. Oglethorpe tactfully spoke against the bill, maintaining that:

> The Pretender has none but a company of silly fellows about him; and it was to be feared that if the Bishop, who was allowed to be a man of great parts, should be banished, he might be so-licited and tempted to go to Rome, and there be in a capacity to do more mischief by his advice, than if he were suffered to stay in England under the watchful eye of those in power.[3]

In 1727, Oglethorpe was re-elected as a member of Parliament for Haslemere. The following year, he was widely believed to be the author of an anonymous fifty-two-page pamphlet, "The Sailors Advocate." In the pamphlet, he expressed great concern about the low wages paid to Royal Navy seamen and the terrible practice of impressment, where men were forced against their will into naval service. The pamphlet also advocated the reform of sailors' conditions in the Royal Navy. Oglethorpe inherited the manor of Westbrook in 1728, following the death of his older brother Theophilus. He was interested in horticulture and, two years later, planted a large vineyard in which he grew enough grapes to make wine.

In his first five years in the House of Commons, Oglethorpe was appointed to forty-two parliamentary committees that dealt with a wide variety of subjects. In 1729, he raised another humanitarian issue in the House when he proposed that a further duty be imposed on malt "as well to discourage the pernicious use of spirits, such as gin, etc, as encouraging

the drinking of malt liquors."[4] He also
spoke that year against excessive royal
expenditure and, in 1730, strongly urged
to increase the size of the army.

Oglethorpe's first connection with
the horrific slave trade at this time was
not a propitious one. On December 3, 1730,
he joined the Royal African Company,
which had been established in Stuart
times with a royal charter. The company
was notorious for having traded over
two hundred thousand black slaves from
West Africa to the West Indies and North
America as the British Empire expanded.

Lord John Percival
(later Earl of Egmont)

However, in 1731, it ceased transporting slaves and from then on traded in gold
and ivory. On January 27, 1732, Oglethorpe became deputy governor of the
company and held that position until December of that year.

Oglethorpe contributed several times to parliamentary debates in 1732.
He spoke in support of free trade by opposing a government bill that would
have limited the trading in sugar by the North American colonies. That year,
he also encouraged the government to support Sir Thomas Lombe's silk
manufacturing factory in Derby, emphasizing that the industry employed
many poor people who would otherwise be without work.

In 1732, he also sought justice and compensation for the shareholders of
"The Charitable Corporation"—a company founded to lend small sums of
money at moderate interest to the poor and larger sums to tradesmen and
others of respectable character upon adequate security. The business had
been defrauded of a huge sum of money, causing great hardship to those
who had invested in it. Additionally that year, he expressed his concern
in Parliament for the plight of Protestant Salzburgers in Germany. They

were being forced to leave Salzburg because of persecution by the Catholic archbishop in that area.

PRISON REFORM

Oglethorpe sat as a Tory in Parliament. At the time, the party opposed the Whigs, led by Sir Robert Walpole, the longest-serving prime minister in British history. Oglethorpe became concerned about the conditions in the English prisons after visiting a friend, Robert Castell, in London's infamous Fleet Prison. Castell was a young architect who had been imprisoned in 1728 for debt and had subsequently died there of smallpox. He had refused to bribe prison staff and was put in a cell with someone dying of smallpox, from whom he caught the disease.

From that time on, Oglethorpe advocated for penal reform. He may have also been influenced by his earlier experience in prison. In 1729, Oglethorpe raised the issue of prison reform in Parliament and was appointed chairman of a fourteen-man committee with the objective "To inquire into the State of the Gaols of this Kingdom and report the same with their Opinion thereupon.[5] The committee was established so that suitable legislation could be enacted. It included Lord John Percival, member of Parliament for Harwich in Essex (who later became Earl of Egmont in 1733), and Thomas Tower, member of Parliament for Wareham in Dorset.

The Gaols Committee of the House of Commons

During the eighteenth century, Fleet Prison was mainly used for debtors and bankrupt people. Prisoners were expected to pay for food and lodging, and the prison was notorious for the cruel treatment given to the prisoners. The Marshalsea was another London prison that housed debtors in appalling conditions. The committee made regular visits to the Fleet and Marshalsea prisons and held many meetings where they examined all aspects of prison life. Oglethorpe revealed their findings in three reports for Parliament—all of which contained recommendations for improvements to prison conditions.

In 1729, William Hogarth painted a meeting of the committee interviewing a prisoner. The picture includes a portrait of Oglethorpe and is in the National Portrait Gallery. The committee's work led to widespread awareness and public approval. At this time, Oglethorpe gained a reputation as a humanitarian and a philanthropist.

The subsequent Prison Reform Act of 1729 resulted in the release of many short-time debtors and a limited improvement in prison conditions

THE GEORGIA PLAN

As a result of the Gaols Committee's actions, many debtors were released from prison with no means of support. On February 13, 1730, Oglethorpe shared with Percival a vision of sponsoring one hundred poor unemployed people to settle in the West Indies. Oglethorpe and Percival then met with Thomas Tower, James Vernon, and others from the parliamentary Gaols Committee and discussed the possibility of using funding from charitable bequests to which Oglethorpe had access.

In 1717, there had been an unsuccessful plan for people from England to colonize land in the British colony of South Carolina in North America. The proposal had been a speculative commercial opportunity to produce silk, wine, and other products for export to England.

The philanthropists had agreed by April 1, 1730, that the charitable funds would cover the cost of establishing a colony there. The committee envisaged that the lands would constitute the thirteenth British colony, which would be situated on the land between the Savannah and Altamaha Rivers in South Carolina. It would be established primarily for rehabilitating people imprisoned for debt. At that time, South Carolina had no settlements south of the Savannah River, and both the province of South Carolina and the Spanish colony of Florida held claim to the land. Spain had claimed Florida as its colony in 1512 and had established several mission stations north along the entire coast of Georgia to Santa Elena (later Port Royal) in South Carolina. The region had been known as Guale by the Spanish. However, these mission stations had been abandoned by the end of the seventeenth century.

South Carolina viewed the Spanish in Florida as a serious threat. Although the Georgia plan was primarily a philanthropic enterprise, the plan recognized that a new colony would also act as a buffer state and protect their Southern frontier. The western boundary of South Carolina reached almost to the Mississippi River, where France claimed lands as part of Louisiana. The whole of the land envisaged for the new colony was known as "the debatable land" because of the claims of Spain, France, and England.

King George II

Proponents suggested that the colony be called Georgia in honor of King George II, who had acceded to the throne in 1727. In 1730, Oglethorpe formed the Georgia Society, composed largely of the members of the Gaols Committee. They agreed that the main purpose for establishing Georgia should be a charitable one to allow debtors from their country who wished to settle in Georgia to do so. The second reason would be economic. Georgia would provide raw materials to England and be a market for English-finished products. The third reason for the new colony was to protect South Carolina against American Indian and Spanish attacks.

THE ROYAL CHARTER

On September 17, 1730, Thomas Tower played an important role in preparing a petition for the associates to present to Parliament for a royal charter for Georgia as a British colony. Prime Minister Walpole was initially reluctant to support the charter because of the likely hostile response from the Spanish in Florida. However, influential members of Parliament who favored it finally persuaded him. In Stuart and early Georgian times, poverty was widespread. The worst poverty was found in London and other large cities, and Oglethorpe and his colleagues would have daily encountered many beggars in London's streets. Richard Burn wrote in the eighteenth century, "There is not a street (in London) that does not swarm all day with beggars, and all night with thieves."[6] This led Oglethorpe and others from the Georgia Society to discuss the wider issue of the plight of the poor in England.

In 1731, the Society agreed that the opportunity to emigrate to America should be extended from prisoners in debt to "the deserving poor." These would be people chosen from the streets of London who did not earn enough to support themselves and their families. They would need to have skills that would benefit the colony.

It took some time for Parliament to act on the request, which went through several revisions. The wording had to include the principal philanthropic purpose for establishing the new colony, while also recognizing it would protect South Carolina from Spanish attacks and enable the production of wine and silk, which would benefit England. On April 21, 1732, King George II issued a royal charter to form a corporation of twenty-one persons to be called "The Trustees for Establishing the Colony of Georgia in America." Fifteen of them would serve as an executive committee called the Common Council, which would include Percival, Oglethorpe, and James Vernon.

The trustees would govern Georgia for twenty-one years, after which the province would revert to royal control. The charter granted the corporation the huge area of land in between the mouths of the Savannah and the Altamaha Rivers and from their sources westward to the Pacific Ocean. To ensure the charitable aims of the corporation, no trustee could hold public office, receive any salary, or hold any land in Georgia.

The charter promised all colonists the same rights as they enjoyed in England, including freedom of worship. The wording stated, "There shall be a liberty of conscience allowed in the worship of God . . . all such persons, except papists, shall have a free exercise of their religion."[7] The prohibition of Roman Catholics to have freedom of worship was mainly attributed to the trustees' fear that the Roman Catholics might be informants for the Catholic Spanish and possibly support them if they attacked Georgia. Although the charter referred to the threat from the Indians and did not refer to the threat of Spanish or French forces, its backers saw Georgia as a buffer against them on behalf of South Carolina.

THE GEORGIA TRUSTEES

On July 20, 1732, twelve trustees, including Oglethorpe, attended the first meeting after the royal charter was granted at the Georgia office in the

The Georgia Trustees' Seal

Old Palace Yard, Westminster. Lord Percival was chosen as the president of the corporation. They agreed that a common seal should be designed with the Latin inscription *Non sibi sed aliis* ("Not for themselves, but others") on one side, above images of silkworms.

The need to raise money was an immediate concern for the trustees, since the charter did not state how the Georgia project would be funded. Parliament initially granted ten thousand pounds but with no ongoing guarantee of future financial commitment. Sufficient funding to the charity was essential and so were ongoing donations by the public. The poor people, who would be allocated land to settle and work in Georgia, needed these funds to pay for their passage to Georgia. A trust store would be established in Georgia from which the new colonists would be provided with tools, weapons, and food during their first year in the new colony.

The trustees then mounted a national publicity campaign. Oglethorpe was enthusiastic and optimistic about the success of the plan and wrote several pamphlets appealing to the public for financial assistance. He emphasized in "An Appeal for the Georgia Colony" that the plan was a solution to the problem of poverty in England. In "A New and Accurate Account of the Provinces of South-Carolina and Georgia," he enumerated the economic benefits of trade with the new colony. Further literature published by the trustees promoted the raw materials and agricultural products, which would be provided by Georgia, as well as the opportunity for exports from English markets. The proposed products included silk, indigo, olives, wine, and timber.

The trustees were concerned that the new colony should become self-supporting as soon as possible. The settlers would become small farmers responsible for equal-sized land grants, since the basis of the Georgia plan was to create a sustainable agrarian economy during the first year of the settlement. Sir Thomas Lombe had advised them that raw silk could be profitably produced in Georgia. On October 9, 1732, they met with Nicholas Amatis from Piedmont in Italy, who said Georgia could produce the finest raw material silk from the white mulberry trees found there. The trustees agreed that Mr. Paul Amatis, his brother, would embark with the first group of settlers and report back to the trustees.

Oglethorpe was particularly concerned that the social classes found in England should not be duplicated in Georgia so that poverty could be avoided. The trustees agreed with this and set strict rules respecting land tenure under the charitable scheme. Colonists could not fully own any land in Georgia and could not buy, sell, or mortgage their property. Women were not allowed to own land, and wives and daughters could not inherit unless they sent a special petition to the trustees asking for an exception to this requirement. No one was permitted to acquire additional land through purchase or inheritance. In addition, the trustees published rules detailing what colonists must do with their land to retain possession of it, including planting and keeping ten mulberry trees on each acre of cleared land.

Although the charter did not mention slavery, the Georgia plan did not allow for slave labor in the new colony. Slavery existed in every North American and Caribbean colony, and wealthy landowners in South Carolina were profitably growing rice and indigo by employing many slaves on large plantations. Oglethorpe did not want large slave plantations in Georgia for pragmatic reasons. He believed the emergence of wealthy owners of large plantations would bring a class divide in the colony. Also, employing slaves would mean there would be less work for the poor settlers who had come under the charitable scheme. A further concern was that Florida had been encouraging slaves in South Carolina to desert to St. Augustine, where they were granted their freedom and formed into a militia that could attack Georgia.

In 1732, the national publicity campaign undertaken by the trustees was very successful. There was great public enthusiasm, and money was donated because of newspaper and magazine articles about the Georgia plan. It soon became possible to send a ship with the first colonists to America. The trustees placed announcements in newspapers about the opportunity to emigrate to Georgia and received many applications. The trustees then established committees to interview those eligible to go under the scheme. That year, the trustees agreed that in time they would also transport to Georgia oppressed Protestants from Salzburg.

The trustees, when selecting prospective settlers, focused on those in financial distress and the individual causes for their situation and at the same time looked for hardworking people who had the skills to make the colony a success. While apparently no actual imprisoned debtors were included in those accepted, it appears likely that some of the prospective settlers were in debt. Sending them to Georgia would prevent their imprisonment for debt.

Eventually, thirty-five families were selected under the charitable scheme. They were required to clear lands, build houses, and raise crops on the land allocated to them. It was also important that the settlers could physically defend Georgia from Spanish and Indian attacks. As soon as applicants had been accepted, the men were formed into brigades and drilled daily by sergeants from the Royal Guards. The charter gave control of military matters to the governor of South Carolina as commander-in-chief.

PART TWO
THE FOUNDING OF GEORGIA

OGLETHORPE'S FIRST VOYAGE TO GEORGIA

On November 17, 1732, 114 men, women, and children set sail from Gravesend in Kent for North America. They traveled on the ship *Anne*, a two-hundred-tons frigate commanded by Captain John Thomas. At his own request and expense, Oglethorpe sailed with them as the only trustee. Reverend Henry Herbert, Dr. William Cox, and Mr. Paul Amatis and his family accompanied him. The settlers included farmers, carpenters, tailors, bakers, and merchants, as well as those with other skills and trades. However, most did not have agricultural experience.

Georgia, South Carolina, and Florida in 1733

The settlers were in the hold, and the two-month journey across the Atlantic was not an easy one because of the size of the ship. Oglethorpe worked tirelessly throughout the journey to care for their needs. One stop was made at the island of Madeira to collect five tons of wine.

In January 1733, the group arrived in Charles Town (now Charleston), South Carolina, where Oglethorpe disembarked. He held an important meeting with Robert Johnson, the governor of the state, who strongly favored the creation of Georgia. Johnson provided animals, provisions, and financial assistance to Oglethorpe to support the new settlement.

SAVANNAH ESTABLISHED

The settlers sailed on to Port Royal. Oglethorpe and Captain Francis Scott left them there and sailed south to the mouth of the Savannah River, accompanied by a small force of rangers from Charles Town. They then sailed around ten miles up the river until they reached Yamacraw Bluff on the south bank of the river. It was an area of high ground forty feet above river level on which there was a forest of tall pines. There were excellent views over the beautiful surrounding area, and Oglethorpe judged it was a defensible position if attacks were made by the Spanish in Florida.

CHIEF TOMOCHICHI

Oglethorpe's priority was to establish good relations with the local American Indians. He arranged to meet with Chief Tomochichi from a small Creek Indian village, which was located nearby. John Musgrove from South Carolina was trading goods with the Indians near to the village. Musgrove's wife, Mary, was a Creek Indian who could speak both the English and Creek languages. She interpreted for Oglethorpe, and he and Tomochichi immediately established a good rapport, which developed into a lasting close relationship. The portrait aside is of Tomochichi and his nephew, Toahahwi.

The Carolina Rangers started clearing the site and built wooden steps to the top from the river while Oglethorpe returned to Port Royal to join the settlers. He sailed with them in six smaller boats for the Yamacraw Bluff. The settlers arrived on February 1 and climbed the steps to the top of the partially cleared rise. (This date became February 12 when the calendar changed. It is now known as "Georgia Day."). The men unloaded what they would need to spend their first night, which included communal tents and bedding supplied by the trustees. While the colonists erected their tents, Oglethorpe set up a small personal tent under four pines overlooking the

Tomochichi and Toahahwi

river. He slept here for around a year. A granite seat in Savannah now marks the site where Oglethorpe pitched his tent.

Oglethorpe's priority entailed building a fence around the settlement as a defense against Indian or Spanish attacks. Some men dug trenches while others felled trees for the fence. A crane was then constructed at the top of the bluff to hoist incoming freight to Georgia. Oglethorpe also began constructing a small fort near the river on which he mounted guns to defend the colony. He organized the male colonists on a group rotation basis to maintain a continual guard. The settlers then started clearing the pines on the top of Yamacraw Bluff. The work was very hard, and Oglethorpe reluctantly hired some black sawyers from Charles Town to clear the grounds and saw wood to build the houses.

On February 9, Colonel Bull arrived with more rangers from Charles Town. Oglethorpe and Bull laid out a plan for the new town, which they called Savannah after the river. Initially, they planned four wards with a grid pattern of wide streets around four open spaces. Each ward was composed of four groups of ten houses for the settlers. The houses would be situated on forty identical lots, measuring sixty feet at the front and ninety feet deep.

On the east and west sides of each square, there would be four larger lots called the "The Trustees' Lots," which were reserved for public buildings. The squares served a military purpose should the town be attacked. Oglethorpe's original ward design was followed for many years as the city grew. It has been highly praised and is the basis of the existing Savannah National Historic Landmark District.

The houses for the settlers were identical clapboard houses, measuring sixteen feet by twenty-four feet with a frame of sawed timber. Under the charitable scheme, each

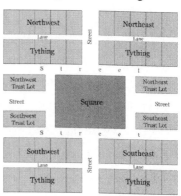

Savannah's Original Town Plan

male colonist was allocated an additional five acres on the edge of town for a market garden plus forty-five acres outside of town for farming the land, making a total of fifty acres. Oglethorpe allocated land for a square-mile common to be situated outside the town fence. According to the size of the land grant, a "quit rent" land tax was due from each settler to the Crown after ten years.

Oglethorpe soon formed the settlers into a company of militia, appointed officers from among themselves, and supplied them with arms and ammunition. He regularly drilled them according to the training that the sergeants of the Royal Guards in London had provided.

The colonists had completed the first house in the town of Savannah by March 1. As promised by the trustees, the trust store was soon built to support the settlers for one year under the charitable scheme. The storekeeper had the discretion to issue food, tools, and certain household necessities to the colonists on the trustees' behalf. He was required to keep account of these items.

THE TRUSTEES' GARDEN

Oglethorpe established a town garden of ten acres by the side of the river and appointed a gardener to care for it. The trustees planned to create a botanical garden in Savannah to investigate what type of trees, plants, and fruit might be best suited for the climate in Georgia. The nursery would supply the colonists not only with mainly white mulberry trees but also with vines, oranges, olives, and other fruits they could grow on their farms. Important botanists gave advice in due course, including Sir Hans Sloane.

Oglethorpe worked tirelessly and enthusiastically on the colonists' behalf during the initial months, supervising the land clearing and the house construction. He also diligently cared for the sick. In March 1733, a visitor from South Carolina observed, "He is extremely well beloved by all his people; the general title they give him is Father. If any of them is sick, he immediately visits them, and takes a great deal of care of them."[8]

During 1733, more ships with new settlers arrived in Charles Town—their journeys paid for under the charity. Individuals known as "Adventurers" also arrived. These individuals paid their way for the journey and were entitled

A View of Savannah on March 29, 1734

to a grant of up to five hundred acres of land under the trustees' scheme. They were required to bring one male indentured servant or family member for every fifty acres of land and hoped to profitably produce crops such as cotton, rice, and indigo.

On May 14, 1733, the *James*, a frigate weighing 110 tons, was the first ship to come directly to Savannah from England. The ship contained supplies and people for the colony. A group of Italian workers from Piedmont accompanied the other passengers at the trustees' expense to assist with the production of raw silk and to train the colonists in the processes required. Paul Amatis had confirmed from Georgia that silk could be profitably exported to England, and the trustees agreed that he should be paid to oversee the production of silk in the new colony.

THE TREATY WITH THE INDIANS

When Oglethorpe first landed, Tomochichi had granted him the right to use the land on Yamacraw Bluff. However, the Indian tribe was a small one, and Oglethorpe judged that agreement was necessary with the other Creek tribes who inhabited the lands southwest of the Savannah River. He invited the Lower Creek chiefs who were stronger and more numerous to Savannah. On May 8, 1733, about one hundred men arrived. Oglethorpe presented them with generous gifts, and for three days, they discussed fair trading arrangements. They also discussed the right for the colonists alone to settle in their lands and start new townships. A formal written agreement was reached on May 21 with the title "Articles of Friendship and Commerce between the Trustees for Establishing the Colony of Georgia in America and the Chief Men of the Nation of the Lower Creeks."

The settlers had initially worked diligently and enthusiastically under Oglethorpe's guidance and leadership. However, from March 1733 onward, the weather got much hotter and humid. Heavy rain fell, and they found the work much more difficult. In addition, once the trees were cleared from the areas outside the town, they found that some of the plots were inadequately drained and had poor soil. Most of the settlers were not accustomed to working on the land, and the conditions in the colony were not as favorable as the trustees' literature had stated.

Settlers at work

On May 31, 1733, Oglethorpe went to Charles Town to maintain good relations with South Carolina. He addressed their assembly on June 9 and spoke persuasively about the need for proper defenses for protection against Spanish and Indian attacks. The assembly promised him eight thousand pounds in financial assistance to provide security for both Georgia and South Carolina.

PROBLEMS IN SAVANNAH

On June 10, 1733, Oglethorpe returned to Savannah following this successful visit. On August 12, he wrote to the trustees that he had found that during his short absence the settlers had become "very mutinous and impatient of labour and discipline." The letter stated that "idleness and drunkenness were succeeded by sickness."[9] Oglethorpe blamed the continued presence of the black workers and sent them back to South Carolina because "for so long as they continued here our men were encouraged in idleness by their working for them." Oglethorpe believed that drinking rum was the basic cause of both drunkenness and sickness, and from that point, he forbade the sale of rum.

OTHER SETTLEMENTS

By July 7, 1733, forty houses had been built in Savannah as per the town plan. Oglethorpe then began to establish many small townships and allowed a maximum of forty lots in each. Oglethorpe granted land that month in Thunderbolt to some new settlers who had arrived in Savannah. A settlement and fort were subsequently built there. He also established a small settlement and fort on nearby Skidaway Island. The two settlements had a strategic defensive role and were reached by boats on waterways. In this area in 1736, Noble Jones established his Wormsloe plantation. Oglethorpe established other small settlements as more shiploads of colonists arrived, including Highgate, Hampstead, Abercorn, Ogeechee, and Tybee. Eventually, a lighthouse was built at Tybee.

GEORGIA OFFICIALS APPOINTED

Although the charter allowed the Common Council to appoint a governor of Georgia, the trustees decided to be responsible for governing the new colony. Oglethorpe had come to Georgia with no formal title other than Resident Trustee and as such, under the charter, could not hold office. The trustees had intended for him to follow their instructions, but in practice, Oglethorpe acted as the unofficial governor. His presence in Georgia was vital. He constantly had to make decisions that could not wait for a four-to-five-month response from the trustees.

Every British colony except Georgia had a representative assembly with the right to decide issues of concern that arose locally. The trustees required Oglethorpe to appoint local officials to fulfill certain roles in the community, while the trustees retained final authority in London. On July 7, 1733, Oglethorpe called a meeting of the settlers and made several appointments. These included three bailiffs (or magistrates) as the chief officials to act as the judges of its court; a recorder whose tasks included summoning juries, administering oaths, and keeping court records; and two constables who were responsible for upholding the law. These officials had little or no legal experience and were given no training for the roles.

Oglethorpe also set up a Register of Land Grants that day. He designated the wards of the town and assigned individual lots to those on the charitable scheme. He stipulated that a town court should be held every six weeks where juries decided all civil and criminal cases, as in England. However, no lawyers were allowed in proceedings, and every person had to present his or her case. The courts were to be held in a wooden building, thirty-six feet long and twelve feet wide. Christian services were also to be held in the building on Sundays. However, once the courts were operational, colonists still came to Oglethorpe with their disputes, and he continued to make decisions.

FORT ARGYLE

On June 18, 1773, Oglethorpe went forty miles west from Savannah into the interior, accompanied by Captain James McPherson and a group of Rangers from South Carolina. He selected a site for a wooden fort in a commanding position on the Ogeechee River. Construction began on the fort on August 1, and it was completed that year in the fall. Oglethorpe named it Fort Argyle, and it became the first in a string of forts he built to protect Georgia from the Spanish in Florida.

Captain McPherson and the Rangers were subsequently garrisoned at the fort, and ten families from Savannah went there to cultivate the immediate area. The Rangers patrolled the surrounding woods on horse, keeping watch for any Spanish or Indian enemies who might be in the outlying area.

Rangers on patrol

THE EPIDEMIC IN SAVANNAH

Sadly, Dr. William Cox, the colonists' physician, died on April 6, 1733. Reverend Herbert then became ill and died on June 15 while on a ship returning to England. Reverend Herbert was soon succeeded by Reverend Samuel Quincy. In early July, an acute, feverish epidemic struck the new colony, and three people died. A total of fourteen colonists died that month of the illness. On July 11, a ship arrived at Savannah containing forty-one Jewish immigrants who were mainly Portuguese. One of the immigrants, Samuel Nunes, was a doctor who immediately treated the sick colonists. Oglethorpe wrote to the trustees that because of the doctor's work, "the sick have wonderfully recovered."[10] The trustees had ruled that Jews should not settle in the colony, but Oglethorpe allowed them to do so. Oglethorpe's decision may well have been influenced by the doctor's actions on his arrival.

The trustees had not found it easy to recruit indentured servants in England, and many of them soon left Georgia for South Carolina because of the hard work in the fields and the hot climate. By the end of 1733, a shortage of them existed in the colony. In early January 1734, because of bad weather and the need for food, a ship carrying forty Irish convicts arrived in Savannah. Oglethorpe paid for them to become indentured apprentices in Georgia. That year, Oglethorpe was thirty-seven years of age and described as "tall, lithe, strong, and one of the handsomest men of his generation."[11]

OGLETHORPE'S EXPLORATION OF THE COAST

On January 23, 1734, Oglethorpe, Captain Ferguson, and sixteen men headed south of the Altamaha River by boat along the coast to explore possible sites for British forts. They spent the night at St. Simon's Island, where they discovered a high bluff with a commanding view of inland waterways. Oglethorpe decided to build a fort there as a defense against a possible future invasion from the Spanish in St. Augustine. The group navigated the coast farther south, and on January 28, Oglethorpe named another island Jekyll Island.[12] He later established a military base there under Major William Horton.

By the beginning of 1734, Georgia seemed to have made steady progress. Peter Gordon, the initial chief bailiff, returned to England for a surgical operation. He met with the trustees on February 27 and gave a favorable report about Oglethorpe's leadership and the situation in the colony. Gordon informed the trustees that about five hundred people resided in Georgia with forty houses standing in Savannah. However, the colony was not profitably exporting products such as silk as had been expected. The colony was far from being self-supporting and needed ongoing financial support from the trustees.

Oglethorpe had initially sent detailed reports from Georgia to the trustees, but as time passed, his reports became less frequent and contained less information. He had failed to send them necessary financial documentation, and the expenses he claimed for setting up the new colony were higher than the trustees had expected. On August 12, 1733, he wrote, "I have been so taken up, what with tending the Sick, what with Viewing the Country, marking out Lands, getting Provisions and Treating with the Indians that I have not had time to write."[13] The trustees grew increasingly out of touch with the situation in Georgia.

On March 3, 1734, James Vernon complained to the Earl of Egmont (previously known as Lord John Percival) that the trustees had not heard from Oglethorpe since December 1733. The trustees then wrote to Oglethorpe requiring improved communications, following which he decided to return to London and personally report to them.

THE SALZBURGERS

Since 1734, Georgia had become known for accepting Protestant refugees from Europe for whom Oglethorpe felt a philanthropic concern. He delayed his departure for England that year to await the arrival of Lutheran refugees from Salzburg in Austria. They were known as "Salzburgers" because they had been persecuted for their religious beliefs in Salzburg. Following an approach to the trustees, they received financial assistance to move to Georgia. On January 8, 1734, thirty-seven families left England on board the ship "Purysburg" led by Pastor Johann Martin Bolzius. The Salzburgers arrived in Charles Town on March 7 and were greeted by Oglethorpe. On March 12, they arrived in Savannah, and on March 17, Oglethorpe selected the site of their settlement—about twenty-five miles inland from Savannah. Oglethorpe laid out a town there which the Salzburgers called Ebenezer.

OGLETHORPE'S FIRST RETURN TO ENGLAND

On May 7, 1734, Oglethorpe left Charles Town for England on the ship the *Aldborough*. Oglethorpe had appointed Thomas Causton, one of the magistrates and also the storekeeper, to take charge in Savannah during his absence. Oglethorpe took with him Chief Tomochichi, Senauki, his wife, their nephew, Toahahwi, and five other Yamacraw warriors. On June 16, they arrived on the Isle of Wight. Oglethorpe traveled to London and met with the king and queen on June 19. On June 21, he met with the trustees who thanked him "for his great care in forwarding the affairs of the colony."[14]

The Indians went initially to Westbrook before meeting with the trustees in London on July 3. The arrival of the Indians caused great excitement in London, and Oglethorpe received positive publicity in the national press. On August 1, 1734, the Indians were received by King George II, Queen Caroline, and other important people. The guests traveled to the king's palace in Kensington in three royal coaches, each drawn by six horses. They subsequently met the

Georgia Trustees with the Creek Indians

Archbishop of Canterbury at Lambeth Palace and visited many of the great sights of London.

All but two of the Indians posed with many trustees at the Georgia office. The portrait aside is by William Verelst. Sadly, one of the Indians became ill with smallpox and died. He was buried in a plot at St. John's Church in Westminster. The Indians then stayed at Westbrook before departing for Georgia from Gravesend on October 31, 1734, on the ship the *Prince of Wales*.

Fifty-seven Salzburgers went with them to join the thirty-seven families in Georgia at Ebenezer.

THE MORAVIANS

A pious Protestant group, the Moravians, had not been welcomed by Lutherans in Saxony and wished to undertake missionary work to the Indians in Georgia. On January 14, 1735, ten Moravians arrived in London following an approach to the trustees. They first met with Oglethorpe and then attended a meeting with the trustees where Oglethorpe spoke on their behalf. The trustees granted them five hundred acres of land in Georgia and a loan toward the cost of their voyage.

On February 3, 1735, the Moravians boarded the ship *Two Brothers* and sailed to Gravesend before departing for Georgia. They were accompanied by forty poor Swiss Protestants who were traveling to Purrysburg in South Carolina. The ship arrived in Savannah on April 8, and the Moravians settled there until they could find a suitable location for their settlement. They were pacifists whose beliefs did not allow them to use weapons, and in later years, an increasing number of them moved to Pennsylvania. Most of them had left Georgia by the early 1740s.

Oglethorpe had been re-elected as a member of Parliament for Haslemere in 1734. On March 10, 1735, following meetings with the trustees, he presented their annual request for financial support for Georgia to Parliament. He persuasively emphasized the importance of Georgia as a military buffer, in particular the danger of the French settlement at Mobile on the Mississippi. The Trust was granted soldiers and twenty-six thousand pounds to build a chain of forts "for the further settling and securing the Colony of Georgia."[15]

NEW LAWS FOR GEORGIA

In January 1735, Oglethorpe successfully persuaded the trustees to promote three bills. They were subsequently approved by Parliament and took effect on June 24. The Rum Act was the first of these laws and prohibited the importation and sale of rum, brandy, and other spirits into Georgia. The purpose was the perceived adverse effects of spirits on the health of both the colonists and Indians. Also, consuming spirits had led to disorderly conduct by the colonists. There were financial penalties for breaking the law, but the new act did allow the colonists to sell and consume English beer and wine. Many colonists, however, ignored the ban. The second law's aim was "maintaining the peace with the Indians in the Province of Georgia."[16] It provided for a system to license trade with Indian tribes in Georgia by requiring all prospective traders with them to pay for an annual Georgia license. There were heavy financial and other penalties for traders who did not comply with the new rules. The third law was titled "An Act for Rendering the Province of Georgia More Defensible, by Prohibiting the Importation of Black Slaves or Negroes into the Same." The sale, purchase, or use of black slaves became a criminal act; the main argument was that slaves would gravely weaken the colony's defenses.

Oglethorpe had arranged that raw silk from Georgia should be sent to England. In May 1735, the trustees, accompanied by Sir Thomas Lombe, exhibited a specimen to Queen Caroline. The queen requested Lombe provide a specimen of fabric manufactured from the silk, which he showed to her that October. She was pleased with the fabric and ordered a dress to be made from it, which she wore in court on October 30 for the king's birthday.

DISCONTENT IN SAVANNAH

Before returning to England in June 1735, Oglethorpe generally kept the colonists happy with the situation in Georgia. However, after Oglethorpe left Georgia, Causton could not emulate Oglethorpe's leadership role. Discontent with Causton's authority increased in Savannah as time passed. "Malcontents," as they became known, particularly resented Causton's position. They were led by the Adventurers, who had come to Georgia at their own expense.

On August 27, 1735, "A Petition for the Use of Negroes" was sent to the trustees—coming mainly from the Adventurers—and claimed that the introduction of slavery was necessary for the colony to survive. The Adventurers had paid for white indentured servants to accompany them from England and maintained that "white servants not being used to so hot a climate can't bear the scorching rays of the sun in summer."[17] In South Carolina, many black slaves were employed on large plantations. The Adventurers contended that black slaves could better withstand the climate and hard work involved in cutting trees and working in the Georgia fields. The petition also stated that it would be far cheaper to employ slaves rather than apprentices. The trustees ignored the petition.

The trustees realized in 1735 that problems in Georgia had been caused by sending settlers under the charitable scheme who had not proved suitable for the hard outdoor work. The trustees decided that when recruiting future settlers, priority should be given to those who had been working on the land in England. They would be informed of the necessity to clear land before growing crops, as well as the difficulty of working in the hot summer climate. They were to be warned about the prohibition of drinking spirits in Georgia and the requirement for all men to be part of the militia to defend the colony.

OGLETHORPE'S SECOND VOYAGE TO GEORGIA

On October 20, 1735, Oglethorpe and 250 new colonists sailed from Gravesend to Georgia. They included John and Charles Wesley, forty additional Salzburgers who went to settle in Ebenezer, and twenty-five more Moravians who went to join the others in Savannah. Two ships were chartered by the Trustees: the *Symond* and the *London Merchant*, both of which were around 220 tons. The ships were crowded with passengers, and once again, Oglethorpe demonstrated concern for their well-being. There was a delay of nearly two months because of the weather, and on December 10, they sailed from Cowes on the Isle of Wight. On January 25, 1736, John Wesley wrote in his journal that "the waves of the sea were mighty and raged horribly."[18] He also noted the care shown by Oglethorpe for the passengers.

On February 5, 1736, the ships arrived at Tybee. Oglethorpe left the colonists on Peeper Island (later renamed Cockspur Island) and went by boat to Savannah. He was warmly welcomed there by the colonists and discussed the new laws with the magistrates. Oglethorpe found there was a serious problem relating to silk production, which had been going well before he left the colony. During his absence, a serious disagreement had erupted between the Italian workers from Piedmont. One of them had spoiled many of the silkworm eggs, stolen the winding machines, and left the colony for South Carolina. Oglethorpe ordered the Italian women who remained to teach the women settlers how to care for the silkworms, to wind the thread, and to teach the gardeners how to tend the mulberry trees.

NEW EBENEZER

While Oglethorpe was in Savannah, the leaders of the Salzburgers visited him with the request to change the location of their town. The area allocated to them had been difficult to settle. They maintained the location was too far from the river to use it for commerce, the land was swampy, and the soil was poor.

On February 10, Oglethorpe accompanied them to Ebenezer, where he encouraged them to remain. However, they persisted with their request, and he reluctantly agreed with it. The Salzburgers chose a spot five miles away for a new town, a spot on a high ridge known as Red Bluff where the Ebenezer Creek met the Savannah River. They called this town New Ebenezer and, after a difficult start, began to prosper. In due course, they were commended by Oglethorpe for being more successful in cultivating the land and producing crops than other parts of Georgia. This was achieved without the use of slave labor. Eventually, Ebenezer led all Georgia communities in producing silk.

Oglethorpe then returned to Savannah, where the people expected Oglethorpe to stay for sufficient time to deal with the ongoing problems that had arisen during his absence. They particularly complained about the conduct of Thomas Causton. The Malcontents accused Causton of having abused both his position in charge of the colony and as the storekeeper. However, on February 14, 1736, Oglethorpe left Savannah and, four days later, arrived at St. Simon's Island. He had brought with him many guns and ammunition for the forts that he planned to build. From now on, Oglethorpe would focus on defending Georgia from the Spanish in Florida.

FREDERICA ESTABLISHED

In 1735, the trustees had agreed that a new town should be built on St. Simon's Island, along with a fort garrisoned with troops. On February 10, 1736, the work began to build a fort on a high bluff that Oglethorpe called Fort Frederica. He designed and planned a town there, and by March 23, a battery of cannon had been mounted at the fort.

Fort Frederica National Monument

Frederica became a principal part of the colony's defense against the Spanish. Oglethorpe also built Fort St. Simons (the Soldiers' Fort) on the south of the island. He built a house in Frederica, where he lived until finally returning to England. It is marked by a small historical marker.

THE HIGHLANDERS AT DARIEN

In 1735, the trustees had been concerned about recruiting new settlers who could defend Georgia. The Highland Scots were Presbyterian Christians with a reputation for being fearless fighters. One hundred and seventy-seven of them, including women and children, were enrolled at Inverness to settle on the southern frontier of Georgia. On October 21, 1735, they sailed from Inverness on the *Prince of Wales* under the command of Captain Hugh Mackay. The Highland Scots arrived in Savannah on January 10, 1736, and after staying a few days, proceeded sixty miles south. They chose a site for their settlement on high ground on the north side of the mouth of the Altamaha River. The Highlanders erected huts for temporary shelter and cleared the site so building could begin. They initially called the settlement New Inverness, but it soon became known as Darien.

On February 22, 1736, Oglethorpe crossed the bay from Frederica to Darien, wearing Highland dress. He was pleased to find that the Scots were building a fort on the site of Fort King George. The fort had been built by South Carolina in 1721 as a defensive presence but then vacated in 1727. Oglethorpe laid out a town there and ordered a sixty-mile-long road to be made between Savannah and Darien. On February 25, 1736, Oglethorpe returned to the new settlers who were still waiting on Peeper Island. They all sailed with him in open boats and arrived at Frederica on March 2, where they initially slept in tents.

JOHN AND CHARLES WESLEY

The trustees had decided that Oglethorpe needed a secretary and the colonists a minister. John and Charles Wesley were Anglican clergymen who accompanied Oglethorpe on his return to Georgia. Charles' main role as secretary to Oglethorpe in Frederica was to regularly report to the trustees about the situation in Georgia, while John's main aim was converting the Indians in Georgia to Christianity. The trustees, five of whom were Anglican clergymen, supported John in this aim.[19]

Charles Wesley

On landing, John Wesley went to Savannah while Charles Wesley arrived in Frederica on March 9, 1736. Oglethorpe warmly welcomed Charles, but an issue involving Charles soon caused serious friction with Oglethorpe. Two women had made untrue allegations to Wesley about Oglethorpe. Oglethorpe then accused Wesley of spreading defamatory rumors about him.

Even though their relationship improved, Charles did not appreciate spending much of his time writing letters for Oglethorpe. On July 26, 1736, he left Frederica for Charles Town, then went to Boston, and finally arrived in London on December 4. In 1738, he had a conversion experience after which he became a popular traveling preacher as part of the Methodist movement within the Church of England. Charles Wesley is better known for many well-loved hymns that he subsequently wrote.

Oglethorpe insisted that John Wesley's main role in Georgia would be to succeed Reverend Quincy as Church of England minister in Savannah. The settlers initially welcomed him, but problems soon arose. Wesley insisted that they follow religious rituals that the two previous ministers had not

John Wesley

promoted. Wesley was also viewed by some as a Roman Catholic. Sadly, when he perceived problems in families, his well-meaning involvement in their affairs was seen as interfering and was not appreciated.

The Malcontents regarded John Wesley as a close ally of Causton, the storekeeper, against whom they held many grievances. Oglethorpe was spending little time in Savannah and failed to deal with the colonists' complaints about the two men. Unlike his brother, John was able to maintain a generally good relationship with Oglethorpe during 1736 until Oglethorpe left for England. However, he was disappointed at not being allowed time to evangelize the Indians.

In 1736, John Wesley became romantically involved with Causton's niece, Sophie Hopkey. In March 1737, she married another man, and on August 7, Wesley denied her Holy Communion. He was summoned to appear before a grand jury on August 22 to answer this and other charges relating to his conduct in Savannah. He appeared several times in court but left Georgia for Charles Town on December 2 before a final hearing.

On December 24, 1737, John Wesley sailed from Charles Town to England. On February 1, 1738, he arrived at Deal in Kent. Wesley met with the trustees in London on February 22, and on April 26, they allowed him to resign from his appointment in Georgia. John, like his brother Charles, had a life-changing conversion experience that same year. He then traveled many miles as a preacher throughout the British Isles where great crowds listened to him. John established many Methodist societies, which eventually became the Methodist church. In 1774, he published *Thoughts Upon the Slave Trade* in which he attacked the slave trade in the British Empire. He supported the abolition movement until his death on March 2, 1791.

BORDER ISSUES WITH FLORIDA

In 1735, the British government had arranged with the Spanish ambassador in London for Captain Charles Dempsey to discuss the boundary between Florida and Georgia with the governor of Florida. Dempsey had sailed with Oglethorpe to Georgia on October 20, 1735. Once they had arrived in Georgia, Oglethorpe arranged for Dempsey and Major Richards from South Carolina to visit Florida. On February 19, 1736, they left by boat for St. Augustine, but no news had been received about them by March. Oglethorpe feared a hostile reaction from the Spanish towards the new settlements at Darien and Frederica. On March 18, while work was underway at Frederica, Oglethorpe sailed south from Fort Frederica toward Florida with Tomochichi and a company of Indians.

On March 19, 1736, they reached an island they named Cumberland Island.[20] Oglethorpe marked out a fort on the north side of the island to be called Fort St. Andrews as a defense against possible future attacks from Florida. He arranged for the Scottish Highlanders to begin constructing it, most of them staying to garrison the fort once it was completed. Oglethorpe planned for another fort to be constructed on the southeast of the island to be called Fort William, which was built by 1740. The next day, they arrived at a beautiful island the Spanish had named Santa Maria, which Oglethorpe renamed Amelia Island.[21] The following morning, they discovered an island at the mouth of St. John's River on which stood the remains of Fort St. George, an old British fort. Oglethorpe decided this fort should be repaired and occupied by Scottish Highlanders. Oglethorpe then returned to Frederica.

Since March 1736, the Spanish in Florida had reacted to Oglethorpe's ventures into their territories by making excursions by boat around the new British settlements. These excursions caused continual alarm to the settlers in Georgia, and relations with the Spanish became increasingly tense. Oglethorpe received information in April that a great number of extra troops from Havana were expected in St. Augustine and that the Spanish were preparing to attack St. Simon's Island. He sent regular patrol boats down the coast and was able to obtain additional troops from South Carolina. In addition, the *Hawk*, a sloop (a single-masted warship), came to St. Simon's Island from Savannah. On June 8, a large boat from St. Augustine was sighted heading for St. Simon's Island. It was filled with soldiers and Indians and armed with cannons. The boat reached as far as Jekyll Sound, but on seeing the *Hawk*, it returned to its base.

Oglethorpe had successfully employed strategies, causing the Spanish to perceive that the British forces were stronger and more of a threat than they were. The Spanish also feared attacks from Oglethorpe's Indian allies. Two Spanish officials came to meet Oglethorpe, and on June 19, he conducted negotiations with them on the *Hawk*. They agreed that hostilities between the two provinces would cease, and a provisional treaty should be drawn up. The treaty would be referred to their governments in Europe to decide the boundaries between their respective countries in North America. Toward the end of September, Oglethorpe authorized Captain Dempsey to agree on his behalf to a formal treaty with the Spanish governor, Francisco del Moral Sanchez. The treaty was concluded in St. Augustine on October 27, 1736.

On May 28, 1736, Oglethorpe visited Savannah, where several complaints were made to him, particularly against Causton and John Wesley. The trustees continued to send hundreds of new settlers, mainly British, to Georgia. However, conditions in the colony became worse as the year progressed. Poor crop yields led to food shortages and poverty. Fear of a possible Spanish attack had led some men to leave the farming and join the militia to prepare for an invasion. This affected agricultural output and led to some colonists leaving Georgia for South Carolina. Sadly, however, Oglethorpe failed to deal with the grievances raised with him.

THE FOUNDING OF AUGUSTA

While in England, the trustees had given Oglethorpe permission to establish a town and fort in Georgia's western backcountry, where much of the trade with the Indians occurred.

On June 14, 1736, he gave orders to Noble Jones, the surveyor of the colony, to lay out the town of Augusta at the farthest point above the mouth of the Savannah River that could be

Life in the backcountry

navigated by ships. A fort was to be situated by the river and occupied by a garrison to protect the town. Oglethorpe perceived the French in Louisiana to be both a military threat and a threat to trading with the Indians.

DISPUTE WITH SOUTH CAROLINA

Since arriving in Georgia, Oglethorpe had insisted on fair trading with the Indian tribes. The Indians in the western backcountry had complained to him about unscrupulous conduct by white traders from South Carolina. The passing of the Indian Act in 1735 meant that traders from South Carolina now had to purchase a Georgia license before trading west of the Savannah River. In October 1735, strong objections to the act were made from South Carolina to the trustees in London. A further complaint was made to the Board of Trade in December, both representations being unsuccessful. On August 2, 1736, Oglethorpe held a conference in Savannah with representatives from the Committee of the South Carolina General Assembly, and a compromise agreement was reached.

However, on December 15, 1736, South Carolina submitted a lengthy petition to the Board of Trade in London asserting both their right to the Indian trade and the right to free navigation on the Savannah River. The trustees opposed the petition on the grounds of the Indian Act. The petition was not heard by the Board of Trade until September 1737 when their report was generally favorable toward South Carolina. The trustees appealed to the Privy Council, who in May 1738 recommended the two provinces reach a compromise. This recommendation effectively suspended Georgia's 1735 Indian Act.

OGLETHORPE'S SECOND RETURN JOURNEY TO ENGLAND

Throughout 1736, Don Tomas Geraldino, the Spanish ambassador to England, had continually protested to the British government about Oglethorpe's perceived illegal incursions into their territory. He argued that Oglethorpe and the governor of Florida did not have the authority to conclude the treaty in St. Augustine in October 1736. The trustees felt the need to hear from Oglethorpe personally about the situation, wishing also to discuss with him the continuing lack of information and large expenses he had claimed. Oglethorpe believed that more troops from Great Britain were essential to defend Georgia from the Spanish and French, and on November 23, 1736, he left Georgia to return to England on the ship *Two Brothers*.

The ship arrived in Devon on January 2, 1737, having survived a terrible storm. Oglethorpe's arrival in London on January 6 attracted national publicity. He met Queen Caroline on January 7, which was followed by a meeting with the prime minister. On January 12, he met with the trustees and reported positively to them about progress in Georgia. The trustees unanimously thanked him and praised him for his service on their behalf. Oglethorpe emphasized the danger to Georgia from the Spanish in Florida, as well as the need for finance from Parliament to properly defend the colony.

On January 25, 1737, Oglethorpe requested thirty thousand pounds from Parliament for the proper defense of Georgia and was awarded a grant of twenty thousand pounds. The trustees received the news at that time that many troops were being sent to St. Augustine from Havana in Cuba. They informed the king of the serious threat to both Georgia and South Carolina and requested a military force be sent to Georgia. The Spanish ambassador in London opposed this request and demanded that Oglethorpe not be allowed to return to Georgia. He repeated the claims of Spain to Georgia and part of South Carolina. However, the British government refused both requests.

Oglethorpe was offered the position of governor of South Carolina, which he declined. However, on June 19, he accepted an appointment as commander-in-chief of all British forces in South Carolina and Georgia. King George II awarded Oglethorpe paid employment in the British army as Colonel of the Regiment of Foot for the Defense of His Majesty's Plantations in America. He was also commissioned to recruit a regiment of six hundred men for Georgia. He immediately began recruiting, and by early 1738, troops from the 42nd Regiment of Foot were ready to sail to the colony. Before the regiment was complete, the government arranged for additional troops to be added to it from Gibraltar. On February 2, 1738, these troops sailed from Gibraltar and arrived at Savannah on May 7.

WILLIAM STEPHENS

In early 1737, the trustees had decided that a permanent secretary was needed in Georgia because of the continued lack of timely reports from Causton and Oglethorpe. On April 27, while Oglethorpe was in England, the trustees appointed William Stephens as First Civil Administrator and their secretary in Georgia to monitor the colony. On August 10, Stephens sailed for Georgia and arrived in Savannah on November 1.

Stephens quickly encountered the Malcontents who sought to influence him about their grievances. He met regularly with them at the St. Andrews Club, where he listened to complaints about their perceived need for slave labor. The Malcontents also claimed that the prohibition by the trustees of fee simple (or freehold) land tenure caused colonists to leave the colony. The Earl of Egmont had noted in his diary on February 24, 1737, that the population of Savannah "totalled 386, without counting wives and girls."[22] In September 1737, forty-four members of a Savannah grand jury sent a representation to the trustees. They mainly complained about the Georgia bailiffs, in particular Thomas Causton. The trustees did not respond to the allegations.

William Stephens promised the Malcontents he would write to the trustees about female land inheritance. On January 19, 1738, he wrote to them, suggesting that daughters be allowed to inherit property and that a gradual transition to full fee simple ownerships should begin. Oglethorpe strongly argued against it and influenced the trustees to defeat the proposal. He maintained that if granted, the Malcontents would then demand even more rights that would not be in line with the trustees' vision. Stephens subsequently lost the confidence of the Malcontents that year as discontent increased because he had proved unable to influence the trustees to support their proposals.

GEORGE WHITEFIELD

George Whitefield was an Anglican deacon whom John Wesley had encouraged to join him and engage in missionary work in Georgia. The trustees agreed he could be a minister in Frederica, and Whitfield was able to raise sufficient finance for the cost of the journey during 1737. On January 10, 1738, he sailed on the ship that was to collect troops from Gibraltar for Georgia and arrived with the troops at Savannah on May 7. By this time, the trustees had given him authority to officiate at both Savannah and Frederica.

George Whitefield

On his arrival in Savannah, the colonists welcomed Whitefield, and he initially ministered conscientiously in the town. Most of the settlers appear to have appreciated his eloquent and emotional preaching. However, he soon sympathized with those who agreed with the views of the Malcontents. Whitefield became particularly concerned about the number of orphans whose parents had died in Georgia and decided with Oglethorpe's encouragement that an orphanage was urgently needed.

Whitefield left Georgia on August 28 to return to England to be ordained as a priest and to raise funds for the orphanage. The trustees granted him five hundred acres of land in Georgia for the site of an orphanage but did not agree to pay toward the maintenance of it. He raised one thousand pounds, and following his ordination, the trustees confirmed his appointment as minister at Savannah. On August 14, 1739, Whitefield sailed from England to Philadelphia and arrived on October 30. He preached powerfully to large crowds in the Northern states and played a significant role in the spiritual revival there called, "The Great Awakening." He raised additional funds for the orphanage from these meetings.

Whitefield left for Savannah, arriving on January 10, 1740. On arriving, he commented, "It was a melancholy thing to see the colony of Georgia reduced to even a much lower state than when I left it, and almost deserted by all except by those who could not go well away."[23] Savannah, by this time, had around one hundred residents. Whitefield obtained a site for an orphanage building approximately twelve miles from Savannah, which he called Bethesda. On March 25, he laid the foundation for the orphanage, which was completed by the end of the year. One year later, the orphanage housed one hundred orphans.

William Stephens and the other clergy were by now strongly criticizing both Whitefield's Methodist theology and the informal services he held in Savannah. The trustees terminated his appointment as minister there on July 7, 1740. In September, Whitefield left Georgia for New England where his preaching to large crowds was more appreciated than in Georgia and Charles Town. He returned to Georgia a month later. On January 1, 1741, Whitefield left Georgia again for England to raise further funds for Bethesda. He arrived in England on March 14 and proceeded to preach to large crowds throughout the country.

From then on, Whitefield was mostly absent from Georgia but supported the orphanage for the rest of his life. Bethesda now exists as a private day school for boys. In the 1740s, Whitefield argued, along with the Malcontents, for the introduction of slavery into Georgia on the grounds it was needed for the colony to survive. However, he maintained that slaves should not be abused but treated in line with settlers who were employed to work on the land. After slavery became legal in Georgia, he used slaves at Bethesda. Sadly, most Anglicans accepted slavery until at least the mid-1700s.

OGLETHORPE'S THIRD VOYAGE TO GEORGIA

In 1738, the trustees became concerned about the need for sufficient ongoing finance from Parliament to meet the continued high expenditure by Oglethorpe in Georgia. They informed him that from then on, less finance would be available for the colony. However, he had obtained the provisions, arms, and ammunition that he needed and left England for Georgia on July

5, 1738. He sailed from Portsmouth on the *Blandford*, having once again been delayed by bad weather. He was accompanied by the soldiers of the 42nd Regiment of Foot, most of whom would be stationed at Frederica.

On September 19, Oglethorpe and the troops arrived at the south end of St. Simon's Island. Oglethorpe camped there for a few days and started building a six-mile narrow road across the island from the Soldiers' Fort to Frederica. It went between a forest and a marsh. He then proceeded to Frederica in the north of the island. Oglethorpe spent most of his time there from then on and was preoccupied with military affairs.

FURTHER DISCONTENT IN SAVANNAH

Oglethorpe arrived in Savannah from Frederica on October 10, where he was warmly welcomed by the inhabitants. However, seven days later, he informed a mass meeting that the trust was deeply in debt and the trust store would have to close. The trustees had also instructed Oglethorpe to dismiss Causton as storekeeper. They had lost confidence in his handling of finances during Oglethorpe's absence. Oglethorpe replaced Causton with a new storekeeper, Thomas Jones. He also replaced Causton and the other two existing magistrates with new appointees. Oglethorpe made it clear to the people that the trustees would not change the present rules that related to slavery and land tenure. There had been an extraordinary heatwave in the spring which had severely affected crop yield. Oglethorpe's actions and announcements in Savannah led to great dismay and widespread concern about the future of the colony. He left Savannah for Frederica on October 25.

On December 9, 1738, 121 settlers in Savannah, including three magistrates, sent a petition initiated by the Adventurers to the trustees that maintained the economic situation in Georgia was serious. The petition argued for black slaves and changes to land tenure so the colony could prosper. Support for change had now become more widespread. Nevertheless, Darien and New Ebenezer both submitted anti-slavery petitions.

OGLETHORPE'S DEVELOPED VIEW OF SLAVERY

In January 1739, Oglethorpe urged the trustees to resist the demands of the Malcontents. He wrote that the introduction of slavery into Georgia "would occasion the misery of thousands in Africa . . . and bring into perpetual slavery the poor people who now live free there."[24] It appears that Oglethorpe's opposition to slavery had by now moved from initially accepting it to being pragmatic and finally to a far-sighted ethical one.

Further unsuccessful representations from discontented settlers were sent to the trustees in 1739. The trustees instructed William Stephens to write a positive report for the next parliamentary debate, and in February 1740, he produced "A State of the Province of Georgia."

In December 1740, the settlers sent further petitions, including one to Parliament. The latter petition also requested "the liberty of choosing our own magistrates."[25] The trustees continued to refuse these requests. On December 2, three of the malcontent Adventurers who now lived in South Carolina published "A True and Historical Narrative of the Colony of Georgia in America." It criticized Oglethorpe's leadership in the colony and was circulated widely in London. The trustees responded by publishing three pamphlets in 1741 and 1742 that refuted the charges that had been made against them.

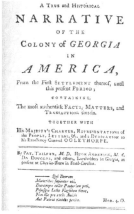

The Malcontents' Representation of 1740

THOMAS STEPHENS AND DISCONTENT

In 1737, Thomas Stevens arrived in Georgia from England to assist his father in running their plantation. In March 1739, Oglethorpe accused him of dishonesty without, he felt, receiving a fair hearing. Oglethorpe's attitude aggrieved Thomas, who had already become sympathetic to the arguments of the Malcontents. In August, he returned to England to represent them to the trustees. However, he was unable to persuade the trustees to change the rules of the trust. In January 1740, Stephens distributed to members of Parliament a pamphlet, entitled "Observations on the Present State of Georgia," that presented the complaints of the Malcontents. However, Parliament still voted money that year to the trustees.

Stephens continued to circulate criticism of the trustees' rules, but once again in January 1741, Parliament voted to give money to them. In April, Stephens left London for Savannah and then in August traveled to Charles Town where he spent several weeks meeting with the Georgia exiles. In late September, Stephens returned to Savannah, where he informed the Malcontents living there of the lack of progress. The Savannah Malcontents then formally elected Thomas Stephens to act as their agent, and he returned to England in February 1742.

The political campaign of Thomas Stephens and representations made by settlers contributed to Parliament's refusal on March 15, 1742, to confirm the trustees' financial request that year. In April, Stephens published "The Hard Case of the Distressed People of Georgia" in which he charged the trustees with both incompetence and deceit. In May, Parliament listened to the Malcontents' witnesses and counsel on three occasions. The trustees' representatives presented their case in June, and most of their arguments were accepted. Parliament agreed there should be a continuing prohibition on slavery in Georgia. However, the importing and sale of rum into the colony was from then on allowed.

Egmont resigned from the Common Council on July 7. He had been the dominant figure among the trustees and had successfully argued in Parliament for annual subsidies. Vernon now became the main figure at trustee meetings. The Common Council had taken no further action in respect of Stephens' allegations, and Stephens continued with his anti-trust campaign. In January 1743, Stephens presented another petition to Parliament, followed by the publication of "A Brief Account of the Causes That Have Retarded the Progress of the Colony of Georgia in America." Thomas Stephens' involvement in Georgia's affairs then ceased, but his criticisms of the trustees, together with the representations made by the Malcontents, led to diminishing financial support from Parliament for Georgia between 1744 and 1752.

THE ATTACK ON OGLETHORPE

In Georgia, Oglethorpe had left Frederica for Fort St. Andrews on Cumberland Island. In November 1738, a mutiny took place by the soldiers garrisoned there who had enlisted in Gibraltar. They were claiming outstanding arrears of pay and the lack of provisions. An unsuccessful attack was made on Oglethorpe's life. Two soldiers fired at him, and "the shot of one entirely missed him, but the other passed between his wig and cheek, and providentially missed him."[26]

THE COWETA AGREEMENT

During the winter of 1738 and spring of 1739, Oglethorpe spent little time in Savannah. It was possible that Georgia might be attacked by the Spanish and the French at any time, and he was concerned about maintaining good relationships with the Indian tribes. On July 17, 1739, he set out on a difficult three-hundred-mile journey to the town of Coweta, where a great council of important Indian chiefs was to be held, both that month and in August. He took expensive presents for the Indians and began discussions with them on August 11. The talks continued until the twenty-first when Oglethorpe concluded an important agreement. It covered their continued friendship and trading arrangements and confirmed the areas of land that now belonged to Georgia. The Indians agreed to stay neutral in any future wars between Georgia and the Spanish or French. Oglethorpe left Coweta for Augusta and arrived on September 5, pleased to find that trading with the Indians was going well.

DEATH OF TOMOCHICHI

On October 5, 1739, Chief Tomochichi died in his village. He had expressed the desire to be buried in Savannah, and his body was transported on the Savannah River to the town. He was buried in the center of Percival (later renamed Wright) Square, where a full military funeral took place. Oglethorpe grieved the loss of his friend and served as one of the pallbearers. A commemorative memorial has been placed in the square. Oglethorpe returned to Frederica immediately after the funeral.

PART THREE
WAR WITH SPAIN

WAR WITH SPAIN

On October 23, 1739, Britain declared war on Spain. It became known as "The War of Jenkins' Ear" after the Spanish cut off the ear of a British subject named Robert Jenkins. The war continued until 1748. Oglethorpe was in Savannah and had previously written on September 27 to Colonel Bull, who was serving as governor of South Carolina. Oglethorpe requested troops to assist in a siege of St. Augustine. He wanted to attack urgently before reinforcements from Cuba could arrive. Oglethorpe repeated the request on October 7 and 20.

On November 8, Oglethorpe arrived at Frederica where he learned the Spanish had attacked Amelia Island and had killed two soldiers. On December 12, Bull agreed to Oglethorpe's request in principle, and on December 29, Oglethorpe sent him a detailed request for the help he needed.

On January 1, 1740, Oglethorpe left Frederica by boat for St. John's River. He took two hundred men with him, which included soldiers from his regiment, Highland Rangers, and Indians. He landed on January 6, and the next day sent the Indians on ahead who burned an abandoned Spanish fort at Picolata.

Oglethorpe then attacked with all his forces and captured a fort at St. Francis de Pupo, where he left fifty soldiers. He learned from the prisoners that the Spanish in St. Augustine were short of provisions and soldiers. He then returned to Frederica. Oglethorpe arrived at Frederica on January 17. He contacted Bull once again on the twenty-fourth urging immediate assistance so an early attack could be made on St. Augustine. Oglethorpe was

Map of Georgia circa 1740

informed that assistance would be provided, and a request was made for him to come to Charles Town. He urgently complied and arrived there on March 26. However, on April 3, he was granted fewer soldiers and financial aid than he had expected. He left Charles Town and reached Savannah on April 5, where he raised troops and summoned Indians to join him.

OGLETHORPE'S INVASION OF FLORIDA

On May 9, Oglethorpe, his troops, and Indian allies assembled on the island of St. George at the mouth of the St. John's River. The next day, they landed on the Florida bank of the river. On May 12, they captured Fort Diego on the way to St. Augustine. Oglethorpe was soon joined by Alexander Vander Dussen, the commanding officer of the troops from South Carolina. The full company marched and took Fort Mosa, which was within three miles of St. Augustine. They arrived on the western side of St. Augustine on June 4. Oglethorpe had planned to mount a siege of the town, while British ships mounted a blockade of Spanish ships entering it with reinforcements and supplies. However, six warships from Cuba were already there, and the British ships were unable to assist. St. Augustine was by now much better defended than in early January.

Oglethorpe divided the troops into three divisions. He and most of them went to Anastasia Island, which was opposite the town and castle. He sent Vander Dussen with the Carolina regiment to Point Quarrel, across the harbor entrance to the island. He ordered Colonel Palmer with the Highlanders, the English troops, and the Indians to scour the woods between St. Augustine and the interior of the country to cut off communications with the town. Palmer was instructed to encamp every night at a different place for safety. However, on the morning of June 15, while the siege was taking place, a surprise Spanish attack took place at Fort Mosa. Palmer and many of his troops who had camped there were either killed or taken prisoner. This was an important setback for Oglethorpe's invasion of Florida.

On June 21, Oglethorpe started shelling St. Augustine. The Spanish returned fire. However, the distance from Anastasia Island to the town was too far for the attack to be successful, and Oglethorpe brought it to a halt two days later. No further attacks were made on St. Augustine. The climate was hot, the provisions were low, and the troops suffered from fatigue. On July 4, Oglethorpe ordered a retreat. The invasion of Florida had failed, and Oglethorpe's leadership was heavily criticized in Charles Town. He returned to Frederica and suffered from "a continual fever," which may well have begun during the invasion.[27] Oglethorpe blamed the failure of the invasion on the late response from South Carolina to his requests for help.

Oglethorpe began rebuilding his forces and planning his strategy for the New Year. During the winter of 1740 and 1741, he built barracks and strengthened the defenses at Frederica. In May and June 1741, Oglethorpe received information that many Spanish troops had been sent to St. Augustine, and an attack on Georgia and South Carolina was likely. He petitioned Parliament on several occasions but was not offered any assistance and felt forced to continue borrowing large sums of money against his estate. He also received no support from Bull in South Carolina. It appears that the failure of the Florida invasion the previous year had negatively influenced Bull's reactions to Oglethorpe's requests.

The Spanish did not attack Georgia during 1741. In late December, Oglethorpe decided to mount an attack on St. Augustine by sea. He set out with two hundred soldiers in two well-armed vessels on a "secret expedition" against the Spanish. However, the force encountered severe winter storms that continued through the New Year, and Oglethorpe abandoned the attack. On January 8, 1742, the British troops returned to Frederica without having engaged the enemy.

THE SPANISH INVASION OF GEORGIA

In May 1742, the long-expected Spanish invasion of Georgia began. That month, a large fleet of ships containing troops and artillery left

Havana and sailed to St. Augustine. On June 20, an invasion fleet from St. Augustine joined the approaching convoy from Havana. The combined force set sail for the Georgia coast with around two thousand soldiers. Oglethorpe received information on June 22 that Spanish ships had attacked Fort William and the British positions on Cumberland Island. He reinforced Fort William but abandoned Fort St. Andrews. Oglethorpe called for reinforcements from the Highlanders and the Rangers. He made a further urgent request for help from South Carolina and sent presents to the Indians with a request for as many as possible to join him. Oglethorpe now had around nine hundred soldiers. Although greatly outnumbered, he is quoted on a plaque at the Fort Frederica National Monument as stating, "We are resolved not to suffer defeat. We will rather die like Leonidas and his Spartans if we can but protect Georgia and Carolina and the rest of Americans from Desolation."

On June 28, the Spanish fleet anchored off the bar in St. Simon's Sound. On July 5, thirty-six Spanish vessels passed by the guns at the Soldiers' Fort and entered St. Simon's harbor. Oglethorpe destroyed the artillery and provisions at the Soldiers' Fort, after which the British retreated and arrived at Frederica that evening. The Spanish troops landed on St. Simon's Island and spent the night there. Oglethorpe sent scouts to watch the movements of the enemy while he made Frederica as secure as possible. The only access to the town was by the narrow road that Oglethorpe had cut through the forest by the edge of the marsh that surrounded the island.

THE BATTLE OF BLOODY MARSH

On the morning of July 7, Spanish forces approached within two miles of Frederica. Oglethorpe rode on horseback toward them with Indians, troops from his regiment, and Highlanders. He intended to encounter the invaders in the woods before they could reach open ground. He soon reached the first party of Spaniards and charged at them fiercely.

Some of them were killed and others were taken prisoner, after which Oglethorpe pursued the remainder for more than a mile. He then posted his troops in the woods, which the approaching army needed to pass, while he returned to Frederica to collect more troops.

Monument to the Battle of Bloody Marsh

This photograph shows part of the Fort Frederica National Monument on St. Simon's Island.

A few hundred Spanish troops came marching single file in the woods where Oglethorpe's advance party lay in ambush. The British troops opened fire on them, and the Spanish returned fire. However, having suffered casualties because of the location and unexpected attack, the Spanish troops returned to their camp at the Soldiers' Fort. Oglethorpe and his troops arrived after the retreat had begun. They stayed for a night near the fort, then returned the next day to Frederica.

On July 9, three Spanish ships proceeded up the river to land soldiers near the town. Oglethorpe sent Indians to attack any that landed, but when the guns from the fort fired at the ships, they retreated to St. Simon's harbor. By the thirteenth, the Spanish were unsure as to what action they should take. On sighting some belated English ships from South Carolina on the horizon, they decided to leave. On July 15, the large fleet containing the governor and troops of St. Augustine sailed to the abandoned British Fort St. Andrews on Cumberland Island. They made an unsuccessful attack on the British at Fort William that day before returning to St. Augustine. On the twenty-fourth, Oglethorpe ordered a general thanksgiving for the failure of the invasion. The Battle of Bloody Marsh, as it became known, proved to be decisive in the war between Georgia and Florida.

On February 13, 1743, following his victory at Bloody Marsh, Oglethorpe was formally promoted to the rank of brigadier general. In March of that year, he invaded Florida for the last time with his troops and a large number of Creek Indians. He attempted to entice the troops out of the fortress at St. Augustine without success, after which he returned in April to Frederica without suffering any casualties.

THE CHANGE IN THE GEORGIA CONSTITUTION

The trustees had decided on April 15, 1741, without involving Oglethorpe, that Georgia should be divided into two "counties." The North was named Savannah, and the South was named Frederica. A president and four assistants were to govern each county. William Stephens had been given little authority by Oglethorpe but was named as president of Savannah, with the magistrates there as his assistants. Frederica's magistrates were to become assistants to a president there, but the post was not filled. In 1743, the trustees abolished the county of Frederica and on July 11 appointed Stephens as the president of the entire colony. Oglethorpe was still in Georgia but had less authority to administer the colony. Stephens and the local magistrates began making decisions without deferring to him. William Stephens continued as president of Georgia until April 1751.

OGLETHORPE'S FINAL JOURNEY TO ENGLAND

Oglethorpe had unsuccessfully obtained funding from either the trustees or the government for his expenses leading up to the Bloody Marsh. He needed Parliament to reimburse him for the large sums he had spent in Georgia, having borrowed heavily against his estate. He was also required to return to England to face a court-martial since nineteen charges had been brought against him by Lieutenant Colonel William Cook. Cook had accused Oglethorpe of "defrauding his regiment by making them pay for the provisions the government sent them over gratis."[28] Oglethorpe left control of the troops in Frederica to Major William Horton. On July 23, 1743, he left Georgia to return to England for the last time on the ship *Success*.

PART FOUR
A BASE IN ESSEX

OGLETHORPE'S ARRIVAL IN LONDON

On September 28, 1743, Oglethorpe arrived in London. However, it was not until the following year that the two reasons for his return were resolved. On March 20, 1744, Parliament voted to reimburse him sixty thousand pounds toward his expenses in Georgia. A board of general officers met on March 24 to consider the charges made against Oglethorpe by Lieutenant Colonel Cook. They found that all the charges were "groundless, false, and malicious,"[29] and Cook was dismissed from military command and service.

James Oglethorpe around 1743

Oglethorpe continued to attend some meetings of both the Common Council and the corporation but became increasingly disheartened. The restrictions he had tried to enforce in Georgia were being lifted, and on November 24, 1748, his regiment there was disbanded. Oglethorpe attended his last Common Council meeting on January 19, 1749, and his last corporation meeting on March 16, 1749.

OGLETHORPE MARRIES ELIZABETH WRIGHT

On September 15, 1744, Oglethorpe married Elizabeth Wright in the King Henry VII Chapel in Westminster Abbey. He was by now a forty-seven-year-old bachelor, while his bride was only thirty-four. Elizabeth Wright was the daughter of Sir Nathan Wright, Baronet, and was the wealthy heiress of the manors of Cranham Hall, Canewdon Hall, and Fairstead in Essex. She lived in the large Elizabethan

Elizabeth Oglethorpe

Cranham Hall on the Cranham Hall estate. It was described as a "beautiful retreat,"[30] situated in the small village of Cranham, about eighteen miles east of London. (The Hall was later rebuilt around 1790.)

Cranham Hall Farm adjoined the grounds of the hall. The Oglethorpes spent their honeymoon at Westbrook, and from then on, they lived in either London or Cranham.

THE JACOBITE REBELLION OF 1745

However, domestic bliss for the Oglethorpes would not last long. In 1745, Oglethorpe started recruiting troops to send to Georgia to supplement those he had left there. However, throughout 1744 and into 1745, fears of a further Jacobite threat from France had been growing in England. The Jacobite invasion began on July 23, 1745, when Charles Edward Stuart arrived in Scotland from France. He was joined by Highlanders on August 9. Charles Edward Stuart marched with his army through the north of England and reached Derby by December 4. However, two days later, he began a retreat to Scotland.

On March 30, 1745, Oglethorpe was promoted to the rank of major general in the British army. He was ordered on September 20 to go north with the troops he had recruited for Georgia. On December 3, they joined the troops of the Duke of Cumberland at Preston. Cumberland was commander-in-chief of the English army and pursuing Charles Edward Stuart's retreating army. Cumberland ordered Oglethorpe to pursue the Jacobites, which he proceeded to do.

On December 17, Charles Edward Stuart's advance troops were at Penrith while the remainder were at the village of Shap. On the same day, Cumberland ordered Oglethorpe to attack the Jacobites when he and his troops reached Shap. Instead, Oglethorpe camped with his troops overnight near the town. Cumberland and his troops reached Shap the next day but found that the Jacobites had left early that morning and were continuing their way to Scotland. Afterward, Oglethorpe stated he had not attacked because he had insufficient troops who were too fatigued on their own to be successful.

OGLETHORPE'S SECOND COURT MARTIAL

Cumberland blamed the Jacobites' escape on Oglethorpe's "lingering on the road."[31] He removed Oglethorpe from military duties and instigated a court-martial. Oglethorpe was charged with having disobeyed Cumberland's orders. On September 29, 1746, the hearing began in London, and evidence was given by witnesses. Oglethorpe was acquitted on October 7 of the charges made against him. However, Cumberland ensured that from then on, Oglethorpe did not lead any English armies, although, in September 1747, he was promoted to the rank of lieutenant general.

OGLETHORPE'S PARLIAMENTARY CAREER ENDS

While in Georgia in 1741, Oglethorpe had been re-elected as a Member of Parliament for Haslemere. On returning to England, he served on various parliamentary committees, and in 1747, he was re-elected for Haslemere. He spent much time from 1746 to 1749 supporting enhanced rights for the Moravians in both England and America. This led to an Act of Parliament being passed on their behalf in 1749. In 1750, he chaired the committee on the state of the British Fisheries, spoke in Parliament during the debates on the Mutiny Bill, and spoke for a bill on limiting the time of military service of soldiers. In May 1751, Oglethorpe spoke on the Regency Bill and in December, took part in a debate on the land tax.

Oglethorpe's friend, Sir Hans Sloane, died in January 1753. Oglethorpe prevailed that year, along with others, in persuading the government to purchase the famous museum which Sloane had built. It later became the nucleus of the British Museum. Oglethorpe spoke on other issues and served on other committees in Parliament but lost his seat for Haslemere at the 1754 election. Also that year, he ran unsuccessfully for the seat for Westminster. Oglethorpe was fifty-seven years of age and had represented Haslemere for thirty-two years.

Oglethorpe's relationship with the trustees had become increasingly strained while he was in Georgia. Sadly, he had alienated Egmont, his close ally for so long. Egmont wrote at the time of Oglethorpe's second court-martial in 1745, "He is an unfortunate man, his vanity and quarrelsomeness rendering him incapable of preserving the friendship of his acquaintance or make new friends."[32]

OGLETHORPE'S EUROPEAN ADVENTURE

In September 1755, Oglethorpe unsuccessfully requested that his Georgia regiment be reactivated. There were no opportunities for him to serve in the British army, so he contacted an old friend, James Keith. He had met Keith when they were both training at the Lompres Military Academy. The Seven Years' War had begun in Europe in 1756, and Keith was now a field marshal in the army of Frederick the Great of Prussia. On October 7, 1746, Oglethorpe decided to go incognito to join Keith in Europe. He called himself "John Tebay" to disguise his identity, possibly because the name sounded like Tybee, the island in Georgia. Oglethorpe was with Keith at the Battle of Hochkirch on October 14, 1758, when Keith died in Oglethorpe's arms. Little more is known of Oglethorpe's time on the continent. He re-joined his wife in England after George III had acceded to the throne on October 25, 1760. On February 2, 1765, Oglethorpe was promoted to the full rank of general and became the senior general in the British army.

THE OGLETHORPES' LONDON LITERARY INVOLVEMENTS

During the 1760s, the Oglethorpes divided their time mainly between Cranham in the summer and their house on Lower Grosvenor Street in London in the winter. Oglethorpe's involvement in public affairs during this period was quite limited, although, in March 1768, he unsuccessfully stood once again for the parliamentary seat of Haslemere.

The Oglethorpe's began to move in London's literary circles. In 1768, Oglethorpe visited the young writer James Boswell to encourage him. Boswell greatly appreciated this visit, and they developed a close relationship. Oglethorpe also contacted Dr. Samuel Johnson, whom he had first met in 1738. Johnson had since become an acclaimed poet, playwright, and essayist. In 1755, he had published *A Dictionary of the English Language*. In the

Cranham Hall in 1789

Oxford Dictionary of National Biography, he is described as "arguably the most distinguished man of letters in English history."[33]

Throughout the 1770s, other notable literary personalities, as well as Boswell and Johnson, joined the Oglethorpes at their London house. They included the painter Sir Joshua Reynolds and the playwright Oliver Goldsmith.

A letter from Oglethorpe to Goldsmith states, "If a farm and a mere country scene will be a little refreshment from the smoke of London, we shall be glad of the happiness of seeing you at Cranham Hall. It is sixteen miles from the Three Nuns at Whitechapel, where Prior, our stagecoach, inns. He sets out at two in the afternoon."[34]

On April 10, 1774, a meeting took place at the Oglethorpes' London house at which both Boswell and Johnson were present. Johnson urged Oglethorpe to write his biography, declaring, "I know no man whose life would be more interesting."[35] Boswell requested Oglethorpe provide them with information so that they could write the story of his life. However, Oglethorpe declined to do so, saying, "The life of a private man is not worthy of public notice."[36] In 1785, after Oglethorpe's death, Boswell wrote a tribute to Oglethorpe which included the following: "I was invited to make one in the many respectable companies whom he entertained at his table . . . In his society I never failed to enjoy learned and animated conversation."[37]

In 1780, the Duke of Rutland commissioned Sir Joshua Reynolds to paint Oglethorpe's portrait, which from then on hung in the duke's home at Belvoir

Castle. Sadly, there was a disastrous fire at the castle in 1816, and the picture was destroyed.

In the spring of 1784, Hannah More, a thirty-nine-year-old notable poet, playwright, and niece of Sir Joshua Reynolds, met Oglethorpe. She subsequently wrote to her sister:

> I have got a new admirer, and we flirt together prodigiously; it is the famous General Oglethorpe, perhaps the most remarkable man of his time. He is above ninety years old, and the finest figure of a man I ever saw . . . His literature is great, his knowledge of the world extensive, and his faculties as bright as ever.[38]

Following another party at which she and Oglethorpe had been invited, she wrote to her sister about a conversation between them and Edmund Burke, who was well-known for his writing, oratory, and political career. More wrote that Burke "talked a great deal of politics with General Oglethorpe. He told him, with great truth, that he looked upon him as a more extraordinary person than any he had read of."[39]

GRANVILLE SHARP

It has been written that "none of the friends of (Oglethorpe's) declining years were nearer to him than Granville Sharp."[40] Sharp was an Anglican and a notable philanthropist and writer who campaigned over several contemporary issues, in particular the abolition of slavery. Oglethorpe wrote to Sharp on October 13, 1776, in respect of the slave trade, "I am exceedingly glad that you have entered the lists in opposition to these horrors. It is a proper time to bring these abominable abuses under consideration."[41]

Granville Sharp

They further corresponded and campaigned together against the continued practice of impressment into the Royal Navy.

In 1777, Oglethorpe produced an enlarged copy of his earlier publication *The Sailor's Advocate*. Oglethorpe and Sharp continued to correspond until Oglethorpe's death. Hannah More, also an Anglican, wrote in support of abolition, and it was the Anglican evangelical, William Wilberforce, who was instrumental in abolishing the slave trade in the British Empire in 1807.

THE AMERICAN WAR OF INDEPENDENCE

The American War of Independence (known in America as "The Revolutionary War") had taken place between 1775 and 1783, after which Georgia became part of the newly established United States of America. In June 1785, John Adams came to London as the first ambassador of the United States of America. Dr. Abiel Holmes later recalled a meeting between Adams and Oglethorpe:

> The general called upon him, and was very polite and complimentary. He had come to pay his respects to the first American ambassador and his family, whom he was very glad to see in England; expressed a great esteem and regard for America, much regret at the misunderstanding between the two countries, and was very happy to have lived to see the termination of it![42]

John Adams later became the second President of the United States.

Dr. Johnson died on December 13, 1784, and Oglethorpe went to a sale of Johnson's books on February 18, 1785. The sketch of Oglethorpe's reading a book at the sale, which he appears to have purchased there, was made by Samuel Ireland. The picture indicates he still enjoyed good eyesight at his advanced age.

Sketch of Oglethorpe

On May 14, 1785, a letter included:

> I dined yesterday at Mr. Paradise's, and was very much surprised at the activity and lively conversation of an old military man. He danced about the Room with gaiety; kissed and said pretty Things to all the Ladies, and seemed to feel all he said as much any young man could do . . . this youthful old Gentleman, was General Oglethorpe.[43]

DEATH OF JAMES OGLETHORPE

On June 30, 1785, General Oglethorpe died suddenly at Cranham Hall of a severe fever, which must have greatly shocked Elizabeth. He was eighty-eight years old.

Oglethorpe was buried in a vault at the thirteenth-century parish church of All Saints, situated adjacent to Cranham Hall. (The church was rebuilt in 1873.) Elizabeth arranged for a lengthy inscription on a memorial to be placed on the north wall of the chancel in the church (see Appendix).

All Saints' Church Cranham in 1872

In July 1785, a detailed obituary in the *Gentleman's Magazine* by Granville Sharp ended:

> His private benevolence was great. The families of his tenants and dependents were sure of his assistance whilst they deserved it; and he has frequently supported a tenant whose situation was doubtful, not merely by forebearing to ask for rent, but by lending him money to go on with his farm."[44]

Two friends of the Oglethorpes corresponded after General Oglethorpe's death. On September 22, 1785, Mrs. Elizabeth Carter, a writer and poet, wrote to her friend Mrs. Montagu, a wealthy London socialite, "I quite grieve for Mrs. Oglethorpe. The good old general and she seemed to be so happy and to have such a cordial affection for each other, that the situation must be very grievous."[45]

DEATH OF ELIZABETH OGLETHORPE

On October 26, 1787, Elizabeth Oglethorpe died at Cranham Hall. She was buried beside her late husband's remains in Cranham church. Underneath the memorial to Oglethorpe were added the following lines: "His disconsolate widow died the 26th of October 1787 in her 79th year, and is buried in this chancel. Her fortitude of mind and extensive charity deserve to be remembered, though her own modesty would desire them to be forgotten."[46] In her will, Elizabeth left the manor of Fairstead to Granville Sharp.

In November 1787, Granville Sharp wrote an obituary for Elizabeth in *The Gentleman's Magazine*: "To her magnanimity and prudence, on an occasion of much difficulty, it was owing that the evening of their lives was tranquil and pleasant, after a stormy noon. Very many and continual were her acts of benevolence and charity; but, as she would herself have been hurt by any display of them in her life time, we will say no more."[47] The wording appears to indicate that the early years of their marriage were difficult, perhaps following Oglethorpe's second court-martial after the Jacobite rebellion and his absence during the years of his military involvement in Europe.

GEORGIA UNDER TRUSTEE RULE AFTER OGLETHORPE

After Oglethorpe left Georgia in 1743, few goods were exported, and the colony continued to decline economically throughout the decade. William Stephens proved unable to exert the same authority as Oglethorpe to enforce the trustees' laws. The sale and consumption of rum had taken place when

Oglethorpe was in England previously and continued unchecked following his final departure from the colony. The Rum Act had not been enforced by the trustees since July 1742. Similarly, land ownership violations increased, which led to the trustees relaxing the land tenure rules. Inheritance and leasing rights were granted, and all land tenure restrictions were finally removed in March 1750.

The employment of slaves in Augusta had reportedly begun before Oglethorpe's departure, and it appears that the magistrates in Savannah and Frederica allowed them to be employed illegally since 1743. William Stephens had begun to favor slavery. The trustees accepted that they could not effectively enforce the law, and on May 17, 1749, they successfully petitioned Parliament to abolish the prohibition against slavery. On January 1, 1751, slavery became legal in Georgia with provisions protecting slaves from certain abuses. Once slavery was permitted, many Africans were brought to Georgia from South Carolina, other British colonies, and the West Indies. In 1752, more than one thousand black slaves were brought to Georgia. A plantation economy like that of South Carolina developed, such as the large rice plantation at Wormsloe, owned by Noble Jones in the 1750s.

GEORGIA BECOMES A ROYAL COLONY

On March 19, 1750, the trustees created Georgia's first representative institution. Sixteen delegates were to be elected to the Assembly from eleven districts to make recommendations to the trustees. It was given no power to legislate for the colony, and the Malcontents were not satisfied with its limited role. The Assembly first met in Savannah on January 16, 1751, and elected Francis Harris as their speaker. However, Parliament failed to vote a subsidy to the trustees that year, and they decided to surrender the Georgia charter to the British government. On June 20, 1752, a year before the charter officially expired, Georgia became the thirteenth royal colony.

REFLECTIONS ON OGLETHORPE'S LEGACY IN GEORGIA

The value of James Oglethorpe's legacy in his time in Georgia has been debated in North America since his death. Earlier historians tended to highlight his achievements and to overlook his failings, while some later writers have been critical and even dismissive of his activities. Whatever viewpoint is taken of his legacy, Oglethorpe certainly was an extraordinary man.

Oglethorpe's independent mind is evident from early on in his life. Despite the influence of his strong-minded mother, he alone of his siblings did not become an enthusiastic Jacobite. After becoming an MP, he was more concerned about following his conscience than about seeking to promote his parliamentary career. He was prepared to vote against Tory colleagues if he strongly believed their proposals were wrong. Oglethorpe was a hardworking Member of Parliament, having sat on many diverse parliamentary committees.

It has been written of Oglethorpe that he was "arguably the first modern philanthropist."[48] He raised awareness of various worthy causes in Parliament before investing a great amount of time and energy in seeking much-needed prison reform. His prison work prepared the ground for later improvements. At this time, he became a national figure, admired by many who supported his humanitarian activities. Oglethorpe demonstrated real concern for the wellbeing of settlers during their journeys to Georgia and when they were subsequently sick in the colony.

Oglethorpe appears to have instigated the Georgia plan. It was primarily a philanthropic enterprise to benefit debtors and "the deserving poor." Oglethorpe was particularly concerned that in Georgia there should not be the same social classes and widespread poverty found in England. The altruistic land tenure scheme was based on agrarian equality. He also supported persecuted Protestants from Europe who later settled in Georgia. Oglethorpe, together with the later Earl of Egmont in particular, raised the profile of the plan to a national level. The granting of the Georgia charter, which followed their work together in prison reform, was a great achievement. Their close partnership was fundamental to the success of the founding and survival of the Georgia colony.

Oglethorpe came from a privileged land-owning background and could have lived a comfortable life enjoying London society. He volunteered to go to Georgia as Resident Trustee, which involved much hardship and danger. When funds coming from the trustees proved insufficient to meet the needs of the colony, he spent much of his fortune to compensate for the financial shortfall. However, his relationship with the trustees soon deteriorated in Georgia. Initially, he had little time to communicate with them but can be justly criticized for his poor administration and handling of expenses while in the new colony.

Oglethorpe demonstrated exceptional leadership qualities when landing in Georgia with the first settlers, and his plan for Savannah has been greatly admired. He had a strong personality, was confident in his own perceived abilities, and could be persuasive in convincing others to support him. He was particularly determined and single-minded and expended enormous energy in pursuing the objectives of the trustees, to which he was singularly committed. After the first year in Georgia, the experiment seemed to have been relatively successful.

However, as the years passed, Oglethorpe persisted with some objectives when it appeared they were no longer viable. This led to increased discontent in the colony. He did not seem to recognize that some of the land could be difficult for successful small farming, a problem compounded by the lack of agricultural experience by the first settlers. He also had not anticipated the challenging summer weather conditions which inhibited working outdoors. This led many colonists to suffer from unexpected illnesses and others to die.

The main complaints of the settlers as they concerned the prohibition of slavery, and the land tenure rules were that Oglethorpe consistently opposed them. Nor would he consider any compromises with them. He continued to retain faith in the principles of the Georgia scheme about land tenure when it was probably no longer realistic. However, after having initially accepted the use of black slaves—followed by a pragmatic approach—Oglethorpe proceeded while in Georgia to hold a far-sighted ethical view of the evils of slavery, which was evident in his later years.

Oglethorpe seemed unable to share decision-making or delegate responsibilities that could have been fulfilled by other people. While he was in England, those who took charge in his absence seemed unable to properly fulfill a leadership role, and after William Stephens arrived in Georgia, Oglethorpe gave him little authority. On his return to Georgia in 1736, Oglethorpe focused mainly on the defense of the colony and did not spend the time in Savannah he had devoted during his first visit. Professor Julie Ann Sweet has written that from then on, "Georgia had too many problems that were too complex for one man to solve."[49] Discontent in Georgia consequently increased throughout the 1730s with the decline in the economy. The representations made by the most prominent settlers caused the public confidence in the Georgia scheme to diminish in England. Their grievances were intractably promoted by Thomas Stephens after Oglethorpe's hasty dismissive treatment of him. Following Oglethorpe's final return to England, the restrictions that had been in force since the creation of the colony were gradually relaxed.

Oglethorpe continued to promote the production and exporting of raw silk even after it did not prove as profitable as had been anticipated. The hope that the colony would become self-supporting financially never materialized. The Georgia scheme proved expensive in the circumstances; and as less money came from London, the conditions of the settlers continued to deteriorate, and many left the colony. On Oglethorpe's return to Georgia in February 1736, the increasing problems were compounded by his perceived need to focus on the defense of Georgia because of the Spanish threat from Florida.

I believe that the importance of the immediate and ongoing genuine rapport cultivated by Oglethorpe with the American Indians cannot be overstated.

From the time he arrived in Georgia, he insisted that all trading with them should be fair. The initial close relationship he developed with Tomochichi was followed by further treaties with other tribes, who demonstrated their esteem and affection for him throughout his stay in Georgia. The agreements concluded by Oglethorpe with the Indians were particularly important when Georgia faced hostilities from the Spanish in Florida. Professor Phinzy Spalding—the late, distinguished, American scholar—wrote, "Oglethorpe not only founded the colony, but by his dealings with the Indians he made certain her existence as a distinct and contributing province inside the empire."[50]

While the charter did not mention missionary activity among the Indians, the trustees favored it. Although Oglethorpe was a convinced Anglican, he saw the role of the ministers in the colony as primarily for the settlers. In general, Oglethorpe maintained a good relationship with John Wesley but denied him the opportunity to evangelize the Indians. Additionally, the colonists did not appreciate Wesley's ministry at Savannah. Oglethorpe also failed to properly support Charles Wesley, who found it difficult to adjust to the colonial situation when he arrived. He was, however, generally supportive of George Whitefield and encouraged him to establish and maintain the orphanage at Bethesda.

Oglethorpe had little military experience before England declared war on Spain in 1739. He confidently initiated an attack on St. Augustine the following year, but the failure of the invasion was widely criticized, particularly in South Carolina. However, South Carolina had not supported Oglethorpe in the attack as he had requested. Since he was possibly sick during the attack, it seems to mitigate his culpability in the matter. Oglethorpe's sensational victory against the Spanish at Bloody Marsh—without the financial support he had requested from England—proved vitally important for the continued security of both Georgia and South Carolina.

The charges made against Oglethorpe at his first court-martial in 1744 were found to have no merit. Although he was acquitted of charges made at the second court-martial in 1745, his apparent lethargy in pursuing the rebel Highlanders does pose the question as to whether this was because of his high regard for the loyal support of the Highlanders in Georgia. There is no question of Oglethorpe's bravery and example when leading British forces against the Spanish in Florida.

CONCLUSION

A justifiable criticism of Oglethorpe's time in Georgia has often been that he failed to ensure that Georgia's economy proved sustainable and that the colony was almost ruined by the time he returned to England. However, the later economic success of the colony when directly under British rule was largely due to the establishment of large rice plantations owned by wealthy landowners who together used thousands of black slaves. This outcome was exactly what Oglethorpe had feared and explains his intransigence in opposing slavery and changes in the land tenure rules. Professor Spalding wrote, "Although Oglethorpe may be faulted for failing to secure the permanent acceptance of the trustees' plan in Georgia, the enormity of the task and the almost revolutionary conception of the colony, in the light of eighteenth-century thought and action, must be considered when all accounts are closed."[35]

QUESTIONS FOR FURTHER REFLECTION ON OGLETHORPE'S LIFE

1. James Oglethorpe's parents and older siblings were enthusiastic Jacobite supporters. Why might he not have publicly identified with the Stuart cause?

2. James Oglethorpe's father and grandfather were military commanders. Following military training in Paris, James fought successfully at the Battle of Belgrade in 1717. However, he did not for many years pursue a military career in the British army. Why might this have been the case?

3. What do we learn about James Oglethorpe as a person from his political involvement from becoming a Member of Parliament in 1722 until he left England for Georgia in 1733?

4. Consider what might be considered as Oglethorpe's main successes and failures during his first year in Georgia. What can we learn both positively and negatively from his leadership style?

5. Why do you think Oglethorpe invited the Native Americans to accompany him on his first return journey to England in 1734? Was it a good idea and, if so, why?

6. What do you think was in the favor of the new laws for Georgia passed by the British Parliament in 1735? In what ways did they contribute to discontent by both the colonists and South Carolina?

7. What leadership lessons can we learn from Oglethorpe's actions as unofficial governor after he returned to Georgia from England in 1735?

8. Do you think that discontent among the colonists in Georgia was inevitable from 1735? If so, why was that the case?

9. In 1736, James Oglethorpe expanded British territory south toward St. Augustine in Florida? Do you think this was justifiable?

10. How successful do you think James Oglethorpe was as a military leader after the war between Britain and Spain was declared in 1739? Identify the setbacks he encountered and consider whether these could have been avoided.

11. How important to the new colony's survival do you think Oglethorpe's relationships with the Native Americans were while he was in Georgia?

12. John Wesley returned from Georgia in 1738 and soon had a conversion experience. His Christian ministry as an evangelist in the UK was subsequently very successful. In what ways do you think his time in Georgia might have contributed to this?

13. George Whitfield has been heavily criticized in the USA for his use of black slaves at Bethany. Do you think this criticism is justified? If not, why not?

14. Consider why James Oglethorpe's attitude toward slavery in the British Empire developed as it did.

15. What do you think James Oglethorpe's main motive was for marrying Elizabeth Wright in 1744? Do you think that it was a successful marriage overall? If so, why?

16. Do you think James Oglethorpe deserved to be acquitted after his second court-martial in 1746, considering Egmont's criticism at the time? State your reasons if so.

17. Consider the relationship between Oglethorpe and Egmont from 1729 to 1745. What do we learn about Oglethorpe's personality from it?

18. Discuss the decisions made by James Oglethorpe during the time he spent in Georgia that relate to his being a convinced Anglican Christian.

19. Do you think the trustees' plans for the establishment of Georgia were destined to fail from the beginning? If so, why? What merit can be found in them?

INSCRIPTION ON MONUMENTAL TABLET IN CRANHAM CHURCH

"Near this place lie the remains of James Edward Oglethorpe, Esq., who served under Prince Eugene, and in 1714 was Captain-Lieutenant in the 1st troop of Queen's Guards. In 1740 he was appointed Colonel of a regiment to be raised in Georgia. In 1745 he was appointed Major-General; In 1747 Lieutenant-General, and in 1765 General of His Majesty's forces.

In his civil station he was very early conspicuous. He was chosen M.P. for Haslemere in Surrey in 1722 and continued to represent it until 1754.

In the Committee of Parliament for enquiring into the state of the Gaols, formed Feb. 25th, 1728 and of which he was chairman, the active and preserving zeal of his benevolence found a truly suitable employment, by visiting with his colleagues of that generous body, the dark and pestilential dungeons of the prisons which at that time dishonored the Metropolis, detecting the most enormous oppressions obtaining exemplary punishment on those who had been guilty of such outrages against humanity and Justice and restoring multitudes from extreme misery to light and freedom.

Of these, about 700, rendered, by long confinement for debt, strangers and helpless in the country of their birth, and desirous of seeking an asylum in the wilds of America, were by him conducted thither in 1732.

He willingly encountered in their behalf a variety of fatigue and danger, and thus became the Founder of the Colony of Georgia; which (Founded on the ardent wish for liberty) Set the noble example of prohibiting the importation of slaves. This new establishment he strenuously and successfully defended against a powerful invasion of Spaniards.

In the year in which he quitted England to found this settlement, He nobly strove to restore our true national defenses by Sea and Land, A free navy without impressing, a constitutional militia.

But his sole affections were more enlarged than even the term Patriotism can express. He was the friend of the oppressed negro; No part of the world was too remote, No interest too unconnected or too opposed to his own. To prevent his immediate succor of suffering humanity. For such qualities he received from the ever memorable John, Duke of Argyle, a full testimony in the British Senate to his military character, his natural generosity, his contempt of danger, and his regard for the Publick. A similar encomium is perpetuated in a foreign language; and, by one of our most celebrated Poets, his remembrance is transmitted to Posterity in lines justly expressive of the purity, the ardor, the extent of his benevolence.

He lived till the 1st of July 1785, a venerable instance to what a fullness of duration and of continued usefulness a life of temperance and virtuous labor is capable of being protracted. His widow, Elizabeth, Daughter of Sir Nathan Wrighte, Cranham Hall Essex, Bart, and only sister and heiress of Sir Samuel Wrighte Bart, of the same place, surviving with regret (though with due submission to Divine Providence) an affectionate husband, after a union of more than forty years, hath inscribed to his memory These faint traces of his excellent character."

ENDNOTES

1 Alexander Pope, *The Second Epistle of the Second Book of Horace*, imitated by Mr. Pope (London: for R. Dodsley, 1737), 4.

2 James Boswell, *Boswell's Life of Johnson*, Vol. 2, G.B. Hill, ed. (Oxford: Oxford at the Clarendon Press, 1887), 351.

3 William Cobbett, *Cobbett's Parliamentary History of England: From the Norman Conquest, in 1066 to the Year 1803. Ad 1722-1733*, Vol. 8, (Charleston: BiblioBazar, 2015), 216.

4 Diary of the first Earl of Egmont (Viscount Percival)" Vol. 3 Appendix P. 34. London 1920-23.

5 Cobbett's "Parliamentary History" Vol. 8 P. 216.

6 Richard Burn, *The History of the Poor Laws: With Observations* (London: H. Woodfall & W. Strahan, 1764), 197.

7 Charter of Georgia : 1732" - The Avalon Project Yale Law School Lillian Goldman Law Library 127 Wall St, New Haven, CT 06511, w.ww.avalon.law. yale.edu/18th_century/ga01.

8 James Ross McCain, *Georgia as a Proprietary Province: The Execution of a Trust*, (Boston: R.G. Badger, 1917), 67.

9 Kenneth Coleman and Milton Ready, eds., *Colonial Records of the State of Georgia*, Vol. 20, *Original Papers, Correspondence to the Trustees, James*

Oglethorpe, and Others, 1732-1735 (Athens: University of Georgia Press, 1982), 27, https://doi.org/10.2307/j.ctv21d63rs.

10 Ibid, 29.

11 Henry Bruce, *Life of General Oglethorpe* (New York: Dodd, Mead, and Co., 1890), 40.

12 Sir Joseph Jekyll was a senior English judge, member of parliament and philanthropist. He was a friend of Oglethorpe's and supported the Georgia project from the beginning.

13 "Colonial Records," 27.

14 John Perceval Egmont, *Manuscripts of the Earl of Egmont. Diary of the first Earl of Egmont (Viscount Percival)*, Vol. 2, *1734-1738* (London: H.M. Stationery, 1920), 112.

15 Colonial Records of Georgia Vol. 1 P. 219.

16 Colonial Records of Georgia Vol. 2 P. 96.

17 Trustees for Establishing the Colony of Georgia in America, "Letters from Georgia v.14201 1735 June-1736 June," August 9, 2022, http://dlg.galileo.usg.edu/do:guan_ms1786_ms1786-14201.

18 John Wesley, *Journal of the Rev John Wesley, A.M.*, Vol. 1, Nehemiah Curnock, ed. (London: Epworth Press, 1960), 141.

19 In 1734, Oglethorpe had arranged for a Christian instruction manual for the Indians to be produced but this was not published until 1741.

20 Prince William, Duke of Cumberland, was the third and youngest son of King George II.

21 Princess Amelia was the second daughter of King George II.

22 Egmont, 399.

23 Joseph Belcher, *George Whitefield: A Biography* (New York: American Tract Society, 1857), 123.

24 "Letters from Georgia," ibid.

25 Colonial Records of Georgia Vol. 4 Appendix.

26 John Perceval Egmont, *Diary of the First Earl of Egmont (Viscount Percival)*, Vol. 3: *1739-1747* (London: H.M. Stationery, 1920), 6.

27 Colonial Records of Georgia Vol. 4 P. 635.

28 Diary of the first Earl of Egmont (Viscount Percival)" Vol. 3 P. 266.

29 Ibid, 300.

30 Thaddeus Mason Harris, *Biographical Memorials of James Oglethorpe: Founder of the Colony of Georgia in North America* (Boston, 1891), 287.

31 Henry Bruce, *Life of General Oglethorpe,* P. 239 line 4 Dodd, Mead, and Co. 1890.

32 Egmont, Vol. 3, 313.

33 *Oxford Dictionary of National Biography* Vol. 30 P. 30 edited by Sidney Lee MacMillan and Co. London: Smith. Elder, & Co. 1892 www.onlinebooks. library.upenn.edu/webbin/metabook?id=dnb.

34 Oliver Goldsmith, *Miscellaneous Works of Oliver Goldsmith: With A New Life of the Author,* Vol. 1, (London: MacMillan & Co., 1908), 320.

35 James Boswell, *Boswell's Life of Johnson,* Vol. 2 P. 351 (ed. G.B. Hill) Oxford 1887.

36 Boswell, 351.

37 Ibid, 350.

38 William Roberts, *Memoirs of the Life of Mrs. Hannah More*, Vol. 1 (London: R.B. Seeley and W. Burnside, 1836), 256, 287.

39 Leslie F. Church, *Oglethorpe: A Study of Philanthropy in England and Georgia* (London: Epworth Press, 1932).

40 Prince Hoare, *Memoirs of Granville Sharp, Esq.*, Vol. 1 (London, 1828), 234.

41 .Abiel Holmes, *The Annals of America*, Vol. 2, *From the Discovery by Columbus in the Year 1492, to the Year 1826* (Cambridge: Hilliard & Brown, 1808), 530.

42 The Packard Humanities Institute, *The Papers of Benjamin Franklin* (New Haven: Yale University Press, 1988), https://franklinpapers.org/framedVolumes.jsp.

43 Harris, 290.

44 Elizabeth Carter, *Letters from Mrs. Elizabeth Carter to Mrs. Montagu Between the Years 1755-1800. Chiefly Upon Literary and Moral Subjects*, Vol. 3 (London: F.C. & J. Rivington, 1817), 252.

45 Harris, 305-6.

46 Ibid.

47 Thomas D. Wilson, *The Oglethorpe Plan: Enlightenment Design in Savannah and Beyond* (Charlottesville: University of Virginia Press, 2015).

48 Julie Anne Sweet, "These Difficulties....rather animate than daunt me: James Oglethorpe as a Leader," The Georgia Historical Quarterly 99, No. 3 (2015), 146.

49 Phinizy Spalding, *Oglethorpe in America* (Athens: University of Georgia Press, 1984), 97.

50 Ibid, 75.

RESEARCH SOURCES

Aldridge, Alfred O. "George Whitfield's Georgia Controversies." *The Journal of Southern History* 9, no. 3. (1943): 357-380.

Altschuler Eric L. and Aesha Jobanputra. "What Was the Cause of the Epidemic in Savannah in 1733?" *Journal of the Royal Society of Medicine* 107, no. 12 (2013): 468-73. doi: 10.1177/0141076813486466.

Arnsdorff, Francis Tannie. "Ebenezer and the Salzburgers' Separatist Identity in Colonial Georgia." *Armstrong Undergraduate Journal of History* 3, no. 2 (2013).

Babb, Tara Leigh. "Without A Few Negroes: George Whitefield, James Habersham, and Bethesda Orphan House in the Story of Legalising Slavery in Colonial Georgia." Master's thesis. University of South Carolina, 2013. https://scholarcommons.sc.edu/etd/1807.

Baine, Rodney M. "New Perspectives on Debtors in Colonial Georgia." *Georgia Historical Quarterly* 77, no. 1 (1993).

Bonner, James C. *A History of Georgia Agriculture, 1732-1860*. Athens: UGA Press, 1964.

Bruce, Henry. "Life of General Oglethorpe." New York: Dodd, Mead, and Co., 1890.

Cashin, Edward J. "Guardians of the Valley: Chickasaws in Colonial South Carolina and Georgia." Columbia: University of South Carolina, 2009.

Cashin, Edward J. "Glimpses of Oglethorpe in Boswell's Life of Johnson." *Georgia Historical Quarterly* 88, no. 3 (2004).

Cashin, Edward J. "James Oglethorpe's Account of the 1745 Escape of the Scots at Shap." *Georgia Historical Quarterly* 76, no. 1 (1992).

"Charter of Georgia: 1732." The Avalon Project. Yale Law School online. 2008. https://avalon.law.yale.edu/18th_century/ga01.asp.

Church, Leslie F. *Oglethorpe: A Study of Philanthropy in England and Georgia*. London: Epworth Press, 1932.

Coffey, John. *The Abolition of the Slave Trade: Christian Conscience and Political Action*. Birmingham: Jubilee Centre, 2006.

Cooper, Harriet C. *James Oglethorpe, The Founder of Georgia*. New York City: D. Appleton & Co.,1904.

Corry, John P. "The Houses of Colonial Georgia." *Georgia Historical Quarterly* 14, no. 3 (1930).

Craig, Winfield Scott. "Slavery and Antislavery in the Founding of Georgia and New South Wales." Graduate school dissertation. Florida State University Libraries, 2010.

Ettinger, Amos Aschbach. "James Edward Oglethorpe: Imperial Idealist." North Haven: Archon Books, 1968.

Fries, Adelaide L. "The Moravians in Georgia 1735-1740. " Raleigh: The Project Gutenberg, 1905. https://www.gutenberg.org/files/570/570-h/570-h.htm.

Gallay, Alan. *Colonial Wars of North America, 1512-1763 RPD: An Encyclopedia.* Oxfordshire: Routledge Publishing, 2015.

"Georgia Colony Founded." Historycentral.com. August 20, 2022. https://www.historycentral.com/TheColonies/Georgia.html.

Georgia Studies Digital Textbook: Student Edition Colonial Georgia Unit 3. Athens: Georgia Public Broadcasting, 2014. https://scetv.pbslearningmedia.org/resource/5aa01c69-c979-4a69-a285-cdb3d5ee4b4a/unit-3-colonial-georgia.

Jackson. Edwin L. *s.v.* "James Oglethorpe." *New Georgia Encyclopedia.* July 20, 2020. https://www.georgiaencyclopedia.org/articles/government-politics/james-oglethorpe-1696-1785.

Lannen, Andrew C. "Liberty & Authority in Colonial Georgia, 1717-1776." Doctoral Dissertation. Louisiana State University, 2002. https://digitalcommons.lsu.edu/gradschool_dissertations/3270.

McCain, James Ross. *Georgia as a Proprietary Province: the Execution of a Trust.* Boston: R.G. Badger, 1917.

McKinstry, Mary Thomas. "Silk Culture in the Colony of Georgia." *Georgia Historical Quarterly* 14, no. 3 (1930).

Parker, Anthony W. *Scottish Highlanders in Colonial Georgia: The Recruitment, Emigration and Settlement at Darien, 1735-1748*. Athens: University of Georgia Press, 2002.

Pruitt, Sarah. "What was the Royal African Company?" History.com. April 27, 2016. www.history.com/.amp/news/what-was-the-royal-african-company.

Ready, Milton L. "Georgia Trustees and the Malcontents: the Politics of Philanthropy, The." *Georgia Historical Quarterly* 60, no. 3 (1976).

Ready, Milton L. "Land Tenure in Trusteeship Georgia." *Georgia Historical Quarterly* 48, no. 3 (1974).

Russell, David L. *Oglethorpe & Colonial Georgia: A History 1733-1783*. Jefferson: McFarland & Co., 2006.

"Savannah, Georgia: The Lasting Legacy of Colonial City Planning (Teaching with Historic Places." National Park Service online. 2002. Nps.gov/articles/savannah-georgia-the-lasting-legacy-of-colonial-city-planning-teaching-with-historic-places.htm.

Sedgwick, Romney. ed. *The History of Parliament: the House of Commons 1715-1754*. Woodbridge: Boydell and Brewer, 1970.

Sloat II, William A. "George Whitefield, African-Americans, and Slavery." *Methodist History* 33, no. 1 (1994).

Spalding, Phinizy. "James Edward Oglethorpe: A Biographical Survey." *Georgia Historical Quarterly* 56, no. 3 (1972).

Spalding, Phinizy. *Oglethorpe: A Brief Biography.* Macon: Mercer University Press, 1984.

Spalding, Phinizy. *Oglethorpe in America.* Athens: University of Georgia Press, 1984.

Spalding, Phinizy and Edward Jackson. *James Edward Oglethorpe: A New Look at Georgia's Founder.* Athens: University of Georgia, 1988.

Spalding, Phinizy and Harvey H. Jackson, eds. *Oglethorpe in Perspective.* Tuscaloosa: University of Alabama Press, 1989.

Sweet, Julie Anne. "Savannah's Out-Villages of Thunderbolt and Skidaway: Microcosms of the Early Colonial Georgia Experience." *Georgia Historical Quarterly* 105, no. 1 (2021).

Sweet, Julie Anne. "That Cursed Evil Rum: The Trustees' Prohibition Policy in Colonial Georgia." *Georgia Historical Quarterly* 94, no.1 (2010).

Sweet, Julie Anne "These Difficulties . . . rather animate than daunt me: James Oglethorpe as a Leader." *Georgia Historical Quarterly* 99, no. 3 (2015).

Sweet, Julie Anne. "William Stephens Versus Thomas Stephens: A Family Feud in Colonial Georgia." Georgia Historical Quarterly 92, no. 2 (2008).

Vickers, John A. *Charles Wesley.* Orangeburg: Foundry Press, 1990.

Wakefield, Gordon S. *John Wesley.* Orangeburg: Foundry Press, 2003.

Wood, Betty. "A Note on the Georgia Malcontents." *Georgia Historical Quarterly* 63, no. 2 (1979).

Wright, Robert. *A Memoir of General James Oglethorpe.* London: Chapman and Hall, 1867.

INDEX

Ambassador International's mission is to magnify the Lord Jesus Christ and promote His gospel through the written word.

We believe through the publication of Christian literature, Jesus Christ and His Word will be exalted, believers will be strengthened in their walk with Him, and the lost will be directed to Jesus Christ as the only way of salvation.

For more information about
AMBASSADOR INTERNATIONAL
please connect at:

www.ambassador-international.com

If you enjoyed this book, please consider leaving us a review on Amazon, Goodreads, or our website.

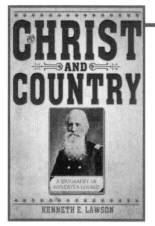

Brigadier General Gustavus Loomis served for almost six decades in the uniform of the United States Army. A veteran of five wars, Loomis was a professional soldier respected by his peers and feared by his enemies. But Gustavus Loomis was more than a career military officer, he was a sincere and dedicated Christian. His bravery in the face of the enemy gave him high commendations, but his real passion was for the Lord and for his family.

A young Canadian working in a New York insurance office auditions to become a regular singer on a popular nationwide radio show–an opportunity for both fame and money. He landed that job, but turned it down because he wanted to sing gospel music. Little did George Beverly Shea know that his prayerful decision would eventually lead him to sing God's word in front of more people than anyone in history. In *George Beverly Shea: Tell Me the Story*, you'll enjoy personal accounts from his worldwide travels as a member of the Billy Graham Evangelistic Team.

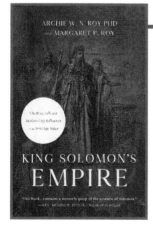

King Solomon is known as the wisest and richest man to have ever lived, but who was this man really? Even though we read his words in the Bible, this man who was the son of "the man after God's own heart" remains a mystery to this day. Even his death is veiled in conspiracy theories. How could a man who was granted his greatest wish by God Himself be so enamored with the pleasures of this world—hungry for sex, power, and more wealth? In *King Solomon's Empire*, Archie and Margaret Roy take an in-depth look into the life of the wise king and the kingdom he led.

Printed in Great Britain
by Amazon

22171768R00066